Dat

TEXAS A&M UNIVERSITY PRESS   COLLEGE STATION

Dat

Tackling Life and the NFL

BY DAT NGUYEN

with Rusty Burson

FOREWORD BY DARREN WOODSON

The paper used in this book

meets the minimum requirements

of the American National Standard

for Permanence of Paper for Printed

Library Materials, Z39.48-1984.

Binding materials have been

chosen for durability.

Library of Congress Cataloging-in-Publication Data

Nguyen, Dat, 1975–

    Dat: tackling life and the NFL / by Dat Nguyen with
Rusty Burson.—1st ed.

        p. cm.

    Includes index.

    ISBN 13: 978-1-58544-472-4 (cloth)
    ISBN 13: 978-1-62349-063-8 (paper)
    ISBN 13: 978-1-60344-608-2 (ebook)

    1. Nguyen, Dat, 1975– 2. Football players—United States—
Biography. 3. Asian American football players—Biography.

I. Burson, Rusty. II. Title.

GV939.N46A3 2005

796.332'092—dc22   2005004658

To my parents, Ho and Tam,

who instilled in me the work ethic

and dedication to follow my dreams in life.

To Becky, the woman of my dreams and

the love of my life. And to Aubrey and

her future sister, the joys of my life.

—*Dat Nguyen*

To my home team: Vannessa,

Payton, Kyleigh, and Summer; always

remember the words of Philippians 4:13.

And to all the U.S. soldiers and

Vietnamese refugees who made it

out of Vietnam, along with the

multitudes who did not.

—*Rusty Burson*

Contents

Foreword

BY DARREN WOODSON

OVER THE YEARS, I've learned that you don't simply watch Dat Nguyen. More often than not, you're mesmerized by him.

I began to realize that the first time I ever watched him play. It was in 1998, and I was at the Dallas Cowboys' training facility in Valley Ranch prior to the start of our season. I'm a proud alum of Arizona State, so I wasn't particularly intrigued by the match-up that was on the television that evening at our facility—Texas A&M vs. Florida State in the 1998 Kickoff Classic. As I occasionally glanced at the TV, however, I couldn't help noticing that the little guy in the middle, No. 9, seemed to be making a play every time I looked up. Suddenly, I was fascinated by his ability to make tackles from sideline to sideline. His instincts were so good that he looked like he had stolen the Florida State game plan.

"Who is that guy?" I asked several of my Cowboys teammates.

"Where have you been, Woody?" they replied. "That's Dat Nguyen. The guy makes plays."

Honestly, that was the first time I heard his name. But as I continued to watch the game, he made an impression on me.

The next time I heard his name, it was prior to the 1999 NFL Draft. At that point, when his name was mentioned, the words "too small" usually accompanied his list of accomplishments. Nevertheless, I was further intrigued when the Cowboys decided to use a third-round draft pick to select him.

The first time I saw Dat at Valley Ranch, I tended to agree with the experts who had labeled him as "undersized." I thought to myself, "I hope this guy plans to play safety, because he really is too small to play linebacker."

Once again, though, I was able to watch Dat at our 1999 training camp, and once again, I was mesmerized. Rookies in the NFL don't usually have "it." Dat did. He understood the game; he understood angles and pursuit; he understood how to make plays; and he understood the amount of work it was going to take for him to make it at the NFL level. Many rookies come into the league with a sense of entitlement. Dat, on the other hand, came to his first training camp with a sense of purpose. I enjoyed watching him work, and I especially admired his commitment to improve every day. He excelled first on special teams, and after that first year, I recall saying to myself, "This kid is worth watching."

As I began to get to know him better, my admiration for him continued to elevate. I discovered that he was as big-hearted off the field as he was hard-nosed on it. I learned that his ability to tackle opponents on a football field was probably a direct result of his family's willingness to tackle huge odds just to make it to America.

I didn't know he had ever been in a refugee camp until long after we had been to training camp together. I didn't know he was the first Vietnamese player ever to make it in the NFL until after I had realized he belonged in the NFL.

But every time I watched Dat Nguyen I was impressed. Especially in terms of the way he lived. During his years with the Cowboys, Dat has made plenty of plays and earned plenty of cheers. But he truly won me over by the way he lived his life.

Dat was almost always the first player to arrive at Valley Ranch every morning. I would typically pull into the parking lot at 6:45 a.m., and his car was already parked and the engine was cool. Every morning, he would arrive early, grab some breakfast, and go to the whirlpool. Then, like clockwork, he would open his Bible and begin studying the scriptures. It didn't matter if he was coming off the best practice of his life or the worst. We could have won our last game or lost big. It didn't matter. Win or lose, high or low, Dat was studying his scriptures. I watched him. Not just as a teammate, but as a brother in Christ.

Honestly, I was inspired by him. Dat truly has no idea how many people in that locker room through the years he has influenced by his diligence in studying the scriptures. I can sincerely say he sent me back to my locker to retrieve my Bible many times. He is not a preacher; nor will he condemn anyone. But his daily ritual of reading the scriptures has inspired many Dallas Cowboys, including me, to begin their day with their priorities in order.

As you can tell, I'm a big Dat Nguyen fan. By the time you are done with this book, I'm certain you will be, too. He's an outstanding football player. He's a super husband and father. He's a great Christian witness, who walks the walk far more often than he talks the talk.

It was a privilege to play with Dat Nguyen. It is—and always will be—an honor to call him my friend. And it is with great pleasure that I introduce to you a truly inspiring story about faith, family, and football; about overcoming long odds and following your dreams.

Dat's worth watching. And, from my standpoint, he's required reading.

CHAPTER 1
Odds Breaker

MY ALARM CLOCK IS SET, but there is really no need for it to go off. My own nervous energy has already triggered my internal clock, and I am eager to get out of bed even before it rings. It's Sunday morning, December 26, 2004, but with all the butterflies in my stomach, I feel like a kid on Christmas morning. All the gifts under our tree were opened yesterday, but there is still something on my personal wish list that I need to get today. It's not something Santa Claus could have delivered; nor is it something that will be on sale at the mall. What I most want today is a win. I want it for myself; I want it for our frustrated coaching staff; I want it for the 64,000 fans who will fill Texas Stadium this afternoon; and I want it for all the Dallas Cowboys fans who will turn on the television and devote three hours of their holiday weekend to watching us play.

It's the last home game of the season, and our biggest rivals, the Washington Redskins, are in town for a 3:15 p.m. kickoff. Through the years, these two teams have collided in some of the all-time classic confrontations in NFL history. The rivalry has featured some of the greatest names in the game: Tom Landry and George Allen; Roger Staubach and Billy Kilmer; Tony Dorsett and John Riggins; Michael Irvin and Art Monk; Mel Renfro and Darrell Green; Bob Lilly and Diron Talbert; Harvey Martin and Dexter Manley. The list goes on and on. Division titles, playoff berths, and Super Bowl trips have been determined by the winner of this game in years past.

Unfortunately, none of those things are on the line today. The Redskins are 5-9, and we bring the same mediocre record into the game. No playoff implications hang in the balance today. Our postseason hopes began to fizzle once and for all two weeks ago when we lost a home game to the New Orleans Saints and then watched a fourth-quarter lead slip away in Philadelphia last week.

Prior to the 2004 season, I had hoped we might be playing the Redskins today for playoff positioning instead of draft order. In 2003, after all, the Cowboys made the playoffs for the first time since 1999, and I believed we would use that as a springboard to make a serious push for the NFC East title. Instead, we endured a series of serious injuries (Darren Woodson, Julius Jones, Dan Campbell, Terry Glenn, to name a few) and failed to win the kinds of games in 2004 we had the year before.

I still look back to October 17, 2004, as a turning point in our season. We were 2-2 at that point and led Pittsburgh by 10 early in the fourth quarter. With about three minutes left in the game, we still led 20–17 and faced a third-and-thirteen from the Steelers' forty-seven yardline. That's when we literally dropped the ball. Pittsburgh recovered, scored the winning touchdown with thirty seconds to play, and went on to the best regular-season record in the NFL. Meanwhile, we lost four of the next five games and began to fade from playoff contention. That one loss by itself didn't keep us out of the playoffs, but with the parity in today's game, one defeat can dramatically impact a team's season. It affected ours in an extremely negative way.

So, according to some of the sports media, we are playing the Redskins today for little more than pride. It's a rather meaningless game, some reporters claim, between two teams playing out their schedule. But tell that to the butterflies churning in my stomach.

Since I first started playing this game in junior high school, I have suited up for hundreds of games. I started fifty-one consecutive games in college, and today's game will be my eighty-first in the NFL. I know the routine; I know what to expect; I know the opponent; and I know that this is not considered a marquee game in terms of the big picture of the playoffs. Nevertheless, I'm still nervous every time I wake up on game-day morning, and I still view every game as a monumental one for me. When the butterflies cease, I will know it's time to hang up my cleats for good. And if ever I get to the point where the next game on our schedule isn't meaningful to me, I will know it's time to move on to the next chapter in my life.

For now, though, I still love the game, and I love this game-day feeling of anticipation, anxiety, and excitement. It's what causes me to hop out of bed this morning, and it's what drives me to my knees to thank God for the opportunity to play today. I don't think God cares who wins or loses this football game—or any other—but I know He loves the participants, and I believe He has led me to this stage in my life. I sense His presence as I praise Him; I feel His strength as I ask for it; and I can vividly see His fingerprints as I retrace the steps that led me to this point.

After my prayers and breakfast, I kiss my daughter and pregnant wife good-bye and take the familiar journey from our suburban North Dallas home to Irving's Texas Stadium. As I drive toward the stadium, the butterflies begin to spin a little faster when I visualize today's game. I have spent this entire week studying the Redskins' every tendency. I know where Washington running backs Clinton Portis, Ladell Betts, and Rock Cartwright like to line up when they are getting the ball; I know where quarterback Patrick Ramsey likes to dump the ball when he is under pressure; I know center Cory Raymer's run-blocking techniques; and I know the favorite routes of tight end Robert Royal and wide receiver Laveranues Coles.

I also know I am completely prepared for this game as I play it over and over again my mind, long before I ever step on the field. I've prepared for the Redskins all week, but I've been preparing for moments like this all my life.

It's just past noon when I walk into the locker room. The countdown to kickoff has begun, and the adrenaline continues to build. I visualize the tackles as I stretch, I picture the big plays as I get taped, and I imagine the roar of the crowd as I begin suiting up. There are far more noble professions than mine: doctors save lives; priests help save souls; scientists make breakthrough discoveries; police officers and firefighters risk their lives for our communities. They deserve to experience what it's like to have 64,000 fans roaring their approval for work performed. Unfortunately, most of them will never experience what I will today. The volume sometimes is so loud that you don't just hear the crowd; you literally feel the fans' energy.

It's now a little less than an hour until kickoff, and after I step into my pants and pull up my socks, I slide on my Nike Field Turf shoes. Today, the "Swoosh" stripe is probably one of the most identifiable logos in American sports. But here's an interesting thing about that symbol: when you or any of the well-known athletes who endorse the company's products lace up a pair of Nike shoes, there's a pretty good chance that the label on the inside tongue of the shoes reads "Made in Vietnam." Imagine that. A company with an image that has become as symbolic of Americana as the National Football League logo or the Major League Baseball emblem produces many of its primary products in Vietnam and then ships them to the United States. During the volatile and controversial U.S. involvement with the conflict in Vietnam, many Americans probably would have had a hard time imagining that they would one day associate anything arriving on a boat from Vietnam with excellence, achievement, and victory. Back then, almost anything from Vietnam was only a reminder of dejection, disagreement, and, ultimately, defeat. From the standpoint of democracy and human decency, there really were no winners in Vietnam.

Yet a prominent symbol of victory in American sports is now mass-produced in Vietnam. Amazing. But then again, fact is sometimes stranger than fiction. And even the most unlikely, outlandish, and farfetched scenarios sometimes occur. The fact that I am here today—in this country, in this locker room, and in this position to experience the roar of an approving crowd—is proof that the improbable is still possible.

Like some of the Nike shoes that now arrive in the United States, I was made—or at least conceived—in Vietnam. My parents were once happily raising their children in a small village called Ben Da, instilling the same values and work ethic in their children that had been handed down to them from previous generations. If there had not been a war in Vietnam—if Communist-backed armies had never left bloody trails through the city streets, the dirt roads, the rice paddy fields, and the thick jungle terrain of South Vietnam—I'm pretty sure I would have been born, raised, and eventually buried in Ben Da. If there had been no war—no National Liberation Front, no Tet Offensive, no Ho Chi Minh Trail, and no Vietminh or Vietcong—I would likely have followed my father's footsteps, making a living along the waters of the South China Sea. Perhaps I would have been a shrimper. Or maybe I would have been selling marine supplies to those fishermen who toiled tirelessly in search of the next big catch. I can only guess at the specifics, but if there had been no war in Vietnam—no fall of Saigon, no napalm, no boat people, and no refugee camps—my life would undoubtedly be so much different than the one I live today.

I'd like to think that if I had been born in Ben Da and raised in peace along the southern edge of Vietnam, I would have been happy with my lot in life. I believe I could have been content following in the fisherman footsteps of my father. That was never an option. The bloody, grisly, horrific conflict in Vietnam was real, and it was a real atrocity for both sides, as more than a million young soldiers and innocent bystanders lost their lives. Many of the men and women whose lives were spared were forever changed. Some survivors, in fact, were faced with a fate worse than death, including a lifetime of horrifying nightmares or a loss of all the freedoms they had once known. As I write today, I don't have a strong desire to visit Vietnam. I don't need to see where the carnage occurred; I don't want to retrace my family's escape route to an awaiting boat; and I don't want to experience for myself a place where so many dreams died and so many nightmares began.

I don't need to visit Vietnam to realize just how blessed I am, either. I have hundreds of reminders around me each and every day. When I lock the doors of our comfortable home each evening, I am grateful that—unlike my parents—I don't ever need to worry that armed soldiers could be lurking in the bushes, waiting for the right moment to seize my possessions and force an oath of allegiance from my family members. When I walk into my daughter's bedroom or look at my pregnant wife, I am reminded that my own life could have ended long before my actual birth. When I crawl into bed each night with Becky, my beautiful wife and the woman of my dreams, I am ever so thankful that my own parents were willing to leave everything behind, fleeing their bed in the middle of the night during the spring of 1975 to catch a boat that might give their family a new chance at life. I don't need to go to Vietnam to be reminded of my good fortune;

my own house is full of reminders that consistently drive me to my knees to thank God for the blessings I now enjoy.

Like those Nike shoes, I was made in Vietnam, but I was delivered in the United States, to overcome obstacles, to beat the odds, and to share a victorious message. I truly believe God still uses common men and women in miraculous ways, and I believe He is using me—an extraordinarily ordinary guy if ever there was one—to show once again that all things are possible for those who believe and honor Him. There's really no other logical way for me to explain my improbable journey from the South China Sea to America's Team. How else could the son of a Vietnamese shrimper end up tackling Washington Redskins for a living? My mother never prayed that I would one day line up against the Tampa Bay Buccaneers; she prayed that her five children and her unborn child would somehow elude Thai pirates.

Some of my teammates and opponents were born to be NFL players; I, on the other hand, was born in a refugee camp to immigrant parents, neither of whom is a smidgeon over 5-foot-2. Imagine the longshot odds in 1975 of that baby boy becoming the man taking the field today.

According to a speech by Dave Ogrean, the executive director of USA Football, approximately 21 million Americans played organized football in 2004. Ogrean, speaking at the 2004 National Conference on Youth and Amateur Football, estimated that nearly 15 million people played flag or touch football and almost 6 million played tackle football. With 53 players on each of the thirty-two active rosters in the NFL, that means that just 1,696 of those 21 million football-playing Americans actually played in the NFL. As far as I know, I am the only person in the NFL who—at the time of this writing—can directly trace his lineage to Vietnam. While there may be a few "showboats" in the NFL, I'm still the only one with a "boat people" background.

When you factor in my lack of early exposure to the game, my parents' size, and my own size (5-foot-11, 243 pounds), the odds of me becoming a starting linebacker in the NFL are astronomical. I may not be able to develop a formula to incorporate all those factors into a mathematical equation, but all things considered, I would say that the proverbial "one-in-a-million" odds are actually rather conservative in my case.

While I am the first player of Vietnamese descent to play in the NFL, I'm certain that I will not be the last. The sons and grandsons of the original Vietnamese boat people are becoming more Americanized every year. With better nutrition, better training, and a better understanding of what it takes to add muscle and mass, today's Vietnamese American kids are growing bigger, stronger, and faster than their fathers and grandfathers ever could have imagined. It would not be at all surprising to me to turn on the television in the not-so-distant future and see NFL rosters dotted with Asian Americans.

When that day arrives, I will be especially proud that I was a trendsetter of sorts. I don't begin to think of myself as the Vietnamese equivalent to Jackie Robinson. What Robinson did for African American athletes—and for the entire civil rights movement in general—is far more heroic and historic than anything I have done. Nevertheless, I have managed to break some racial barriers and cross some lines that had never before been traversed. That has made me recognizable among the rapidly increasing Asian population in this country. I'm proud of my family's heritage, and I consider it an honor to potentially serve as a role model to any Asian American youth who dream of filling my shoes in the future. I only hope that their road has been made easier by some of the obstacles I have overcome.

Back when I first began playing organized sports, the Vietnamese—even law-abiding, hard-working Vietnamese—often represented only a reminder of a dark time in American history.

The hatred the immigrants experienced in the United States was misguided, but it was hatred nonetheless. I learned when to take a stand, when to fight, and when to run. I learned how to find a middle ground without compromising my Christian faith or values. I learned about racism and prejudice, and I learned how to force a smile when people "fondly" referred to me as "chink," "gook," or "slant eyes." I learned how to be bold without being brash. I learned that fighting injustices is often best done without ever raising a fist and that teaching with actions is usually much more effective than preaching with words.

Most of all, though, I learned how to tackle life head-on without succumbing to fear, failures, difficult circumstances, or anything else that could be perceived as an obstacle. That's primarily why I wanted to write this book. I believe the obstacles my family and I have overcome can serve as an inspiration to others. Not just to other Asian Americans, but to all those who have ever been told that their dreams are foolish or that their genetic makeup is simply not sufficient to achieve their goals.

Don't believe it. Walk a mile in my shoes—the ones made in Vietnam—and I believe you will clearly see that my so-called road to success was paved with plenty of potholes, detours, and even a few apparent roadblocks. But with each wrong turn or diversion I encountered, I refused to believe that the road had come to an end—that there was no other way to reach my desired destination. In that regard, my story is probably as much about hardheadedness as it is about good luck. But I also believe that each of the obstacles I encountered along the way made me stronger, increasing my resolve, toughening my skin, and enhancing my focus. I believe everything happens for a reason. Not just the good things, not just the enjoyable things, but everything.

I first learned how to play football when I was in the eighth grade. My parents didn't even know I was playing at the time, and I didn't finally break down and tell them until I came home one day with a broken arm. They were not pleased, and they did not particularly encourage my pursuit of gridiron glory. Even by the time I became a fairly big regional name at Rockport-Fulton High School along the Texas Gulf Coast, they weren't big fans of my football dreams. They attended only two of my games in high school—both on Parents' Night—and they left each game before the first quarter ever ended. I don't mention that to criticize my parents. On the contrary, I consider them two of my most influential role models. They simply didn't understand my dreams—or my game—and they couldn't fathom how far those dreams would end up taking me.

You might know the feeling. When someone close to you doesn't understand your visions or buy into your plans, it can be demoralizing. But I've learned that you don't need people constantly patting you on the back or feeding your ego to propel you to bigger things. Long before I experienced the sensation of hearing fans saluting my name, I heard the taunting voices of those who didn't want me to succeed. It didn't derail me. It probably added fuel to my competitive fire. It was also good practice for all the future obstacles I would encounter.

I didn't hear any racist taunts when I first arrived at Texas A&M. I did, however, hear the whispers, as coaches and players wondered why on earth I—short and overweight for my size—had ever been awarded a scholarship. After proving myself in college, I again heard all the comments about being too small to make it in the pros. When Bill Parcells became the head coach of the Dallas Cowboys prior to the 2003 season, I was constantly reminded that I didn't fit the massive mold of the Parcells-type middle linebacker. Yet, despite all the doubts I faced heading into the 2003 season, I led the Cowboys in tackles and was voted by the Associated Press as a second-team All-Pro at the conclusion of that season. Based largely on what I had done in 2003, my teammates elected me to serve as the defensive captain during the 2004 season. From the Indochinese peninsula in Southeast Asia to captain of America's Team . . . imagine the odds of that.

I'm proud of the obstacles I have overcome and some of the individual accolades I have received. I'm also proud to be the first player of Vietnamese descent to play in the NFL. From a football perspective, though, I am probably most proud of the fact that my teammates and coaches inside this locker room today no longer view me as the Vietnamese American linebacker. They view me, for the most part, as a dependable teammate. I've earned their respect because of my work ethic, not my ethnicity. Inside an NFL locker room, guys care a heck of a lot more about your backbone than your background, and through my first six years in the NFL, I've proven that I can make plays on Sundays.

That's what I am visualizing I will do in today's game as we leave the locker room, walk down the tunnel, and run onto the field for the opening kickoff. I still get chills when I step onto the field and hear the first roar of the crowd. I still play every game with the knowledge that, because of injuries, this could easily be the last one I ever play. And I still feel a sincere appreciation for the opportunity to make a living doing what I love. I know hundreds of thousands of men would like to be in my Nike shoes today, and even though the playoffs aren't on the line, I am determined to lay it on the line every play.

Entering the fourth quarter, we hold a precarious 6–3 lead. Early in the final quarter, however, the Redskins march eighty yards in thirteen plays to take a 10–6 advantage. Our offense fails to move the ball during its next three possessions, and with 1:46 left in the game the Redskins take over at their own thirty-three. As a defense, we know that one first down is all Washington needs to run out the clock and go home with a win. The media may have dubbed this a meaningless game, but inside our huddle, the intensity is nearing playoff level. We stop the

Redskins on three plays, forcing a punt that gives our offense one more chance with 1:25 left in the contest. The offense overcomes a fourth-and-ten situation deep in our own territory, and with just 37 seconds left, Vinny Testeverde hits Patrick Crayton on a thirty-nine-yard touchdown pass. The Redskins then miss a fifty-seven-yard field goal attempt on the game's final play to give us a much-needed 13–10 win.

Driving home after the game, I think back to all the plays I could have made. I think of the things I wish I had done differently, and I recall the mistakes that could have been prevented. Despite some individual disappointments, however, I am thrilled to have been a part of a win. Our team needed it, and our fans deserved it.

Unfortunately, we weren't able to build on it. We lost the season finale to the Giants in New York to finish 6-10. As I've already said, though, I believe everything happens for a reason. Maybe we needed a dose of reality in 2004 to help us realize dreams in the future. Maybe our record in 2004 was the key to securing draft picks who will play instrumental roles in leading this team back to the Super Bowl in the near future. Considering all of our recent struggles with the Cowboys, even mentioning the Super Bowl may sound like a preposterous statement. But consider the source. The mere fact that I am part of this team is proof that the most unlikely, outlandish, and far-fetched scenarios sometimes occur, and I will not stop believing there is a Super Bowl in my future until either we get there or I am no longer under an NFL contract.

My current contract with the Cowboys runs through the 2007 season, and—God willing—I hope to still be plugging away, making plays, scrutinizing myself, and helping the Cowboys make a return to their glorious past until that time. But even if my career ends without a Pro Bowl, a Super Bowl, or even a playoff victory, I am already ever so grateful for all that God has blessed me with on this adventurous journey. I am rarely satisfied when I replay a game, but when I replay the sequence of events that led me to this point in my life, I am content beyond my wildest expectations. Quite frankly, as I kiss my wife, hold my daughter, and look at myself in the mirror, I am amazed that I have been so richly rewarded for displaying a little faith, spilling a lot of sweat, and refusing to believe that I could not accomplish something merely because someone doubted me or said that I couldn't.

You may have picked up this book because you admire the way I tackle on a football field. Over the next eleven chapters, I hope you also see that I have approached my life in much the same manner as I play the game. Football is not my sole purpose in life, but it has become a metaphor for my life's story. I tackle. That's what I do; that's who I am. I tackle running backs, quarterbacks, and wide receivers on the field, and I attempt to tackle obstacles off the field with the same passion and intensity I try to display between the lines. As you read this book, I also hope you come to the conclusion that if a little Vietnamese kid can overcome astronomical odds to make it to the NFL, you can achieve seemingly farfetched dreams, as well. It may require rivers of sweat, pools of blood, and going the extra mile. But when you lace up your Nikes to go the distance, check out the label on the tongue of your shoes and think of me.

That label just may happen to say, "Made in Vietnam." What would have been the odds of that?

CHAPTER 2
Village People

IT'S DIFFICULT TO DESCRIBE the emotions that suddenly overcame me when I opened the letter. It was my senior season at Texas A&M, and as I scanned the scathing words, a mixture of shock, disbelief, anger, and perhaps even a little uneasiness rushed through me. Chills went down my spine as I realized that the bottom-line message, according to the letter's author, was that I didn't deserve to live.

It's not uncommon—now or then—for me to receive plenty of mail from people I do not know. Most of the letters I get come from well-wishing fans, congratulating me on a big game or requesting my appearance. Many others ask for autographs on anything from a picture to a Range Rover. (Seriously, a wealthy A&M alumnus once asked me to sign the leather seats of his brand-new $70,000 Range Rover. But that's another story.) Anyway, in October of 1998, I opened this particular letter, which included a return address, with no reservations. But I was shaken, to say the least, as I read its hostile tone and menacing message.

Written by a man whose brother was killed in Vietnam, the letter, in no uncertain terms, stated that I did not deserve to be living after what had happened to his brother in Vietnam. I was concerned enough that I first turned the letter over to our strength and conditioning coach at A&M, Mike Clark. Mike was much more than a coach to me; he was—and is—a close personal friend. When I handed the letter to Coach Clark, I could tell by the look on his face that he was ready to go find the guy and rip his lungs out. In fact, he later told me that was his first thought about how he should handle the situation. I assure you Coach Clark would be more than capable of doing just that. At the time, he was forty-four going on twenty-two physically. Unlike many other strength coaches out there, he doesn't just talk a big game. He backs up his instructions with a sculpted physique to prove that he knows what he's talking about.

After overcoming his initial urge to retaliate by turning this person into a punching bag, however, Coach Clark composed himself and asked me if he could keep the letter. He took it to Mike Ragan, the head of Texas A&M's team security and a 1985 graduate of the FBI National Academy. Ragan checked in with his contacts at the FBI, and at least an informal investigation began. The investigation determined that the writer of the letter did indeed live at the return address he had included on the letter. It also determined he wasn't a mentally deranged serial killer. I was told I had nothing to worry about, because he didn't have a criminal background that would lead authorities to believe he was a threat. Nevertheless, the content of the letter bothered me.

I simply couldn't understand the author's line of thinking, suggesting that I didn't deserve to live. My heartfelt sentiments go out to this man and every other person who lost loved ones fighting a war in Vietnam. The Vietnam Veterans Memorial in Washington, D.C., hits me just as hard as it hits my white and black friends. Maybe harder. When I think of the tens of thousands of names on that wall, I am heartbroken for the family members they left behind. They are not just names; they were young men and women with dreams, future plans, families, commitments, and goals. The devastating terrorist attacks on September 11, 2001, took the lives of more than three thousand people and sent shockwaves of grief across the country. It was a tragedy that affected us all. But to put the war in Vietnam into perspective, the battles there took fifty-eight thousand American lives, which would be the equivalent of more than nineteen September 11s. When I visualize the horrors those soldiers must have encountered in Vietnam, the blood they shed, and the pain they endured, I am taken aback. Their sacrifices are much more heroic than most of us will ever know. I think of the children who never knew their fathers. I hurt for the mothers, fathers, and wives whose lives have never been the same. Perhaps most of all, I sympathize with those Vietnam veterans who made it back only to face hostilities at home and a lifetime of haunting memories.

But if I don't deserve to live, didn't they all fight and die in vain? Books, movie scripts, and college theses have been written about why the United States became involved in the war in Vietnam. To be perfectly honest, I don't know the full origins, and I certainly don't understand all the political reasons behind it. Perhaps one day I will sort through the Pentagon Papers to obtain for myself a more educated assessment and history of the conflict in Vietnam. Until then, I choose to believe that those American soldiers who were killed in Vietnam died valiantly fighting for the very principles that the founding fathers of the United States cited in 1776. Maybe I'm too simplistic and naive. But if those soldiers were willing to fight for the principles of the United States' democratic system, I believe it is my duty to live my life in an honorable pursuit of those self-evident truths.

Vietnam is viewed much differently than most battles in U.S. history. I've read some things about the conspiracy theories, the cover-ups, and the scandals of politicians during the Vietnam conflict. I've heard about ulterior motives, lies, and corruption. But no matter what actually transpired behind political closed doors, I believe the American soldiers who fought in Vietnam did so with the purest intentions of protecting freedom. That's the point Mike Clark made to me when I brought this particular letter to him. It's also the point Mike tried to make to the author of the letter when he wrote this back to him:

Dear Mr. ——:

My name is Mike Clark. I am the strength and conditioning coach at Texas A&M. I have been very blessed to have a close and personal relationship with Dat Nguyen. It is because of that relationship that I was able to read your letter. I cannot express my sorrow for the loss of your brother. I too lost someone very close to me in the Vietnam war. I can relate to your feelings of anger and frustration about the loss of a loved one.

I do feel, however, that your anger is misplaced. Your brother went to war to protect freedom. Freedom for all people, not just those who were blessed enough to be born in this country. I find it interesting that your last name is Irish. Most likely, your ancestors came to this country fleeing from oppression and seeking freedom. This is the exact same thing that Dat's family did some twenty years ago.

I hope that you can overcome your hatred in time. It serves no purpose and is doing you much harm and robbing you of so much joy in your life. Your brother's death was not in vain, because of his sense of duty to our great nation. A nation made up of many different kinds of people, yet people looking for the same things: Life, Liberty, and the pursuit of happiness. I wish you all the best, just as I hope for nothing but the best for Dat and his family.

Neither Mike nor I ever heard back from the letter's author. But I do hope Mike's letter made an impression on him. It certainly did on me. For me, it was a reaffirmation that I am 100 percent American and 100 percent entitled to the "American Dream." This, after all, is a nation founded on immigration. The inscription by Emma Lazarus on the Statue of Liberty reads:

> ... *Give me your tired, your poor,*
> *Your huddled masses yearning to breathe free,*
> *The wretched refuse of your teeming shore;*
> *Send these, the homeless, tempest-tost to me.*
> *I lift my lamp beside the golden door!*

Of course, that applies to my family and every other Vietnamese refugee who escaped the atrocities of their native land for a new life in the United States—just as it applied to the Irish, Italian, African, and German immigrants who arrived before. In fact, the Statue of Liberty—the very symbol of American freedom—is an immigrant of sorts, designed by a French sculptor and given by the French people.

I, on the other hand, was born in America. I was raised as much on hot dogs and apple pie as I was on rice and egg rolls. I am proud to be a red-blooded, Old Glory–waving American. But maybe most of all, I am proud to represent the American ideal that freedom—here and abroad—is worth fighting and dying for. Beyond any doubt, I'm convinced I am here today because of two reasons—God's grace and America's ideology. I am eternally thankful to God for the gifts, opportunities, and abilities He has provided me. And I am ever so grateful that American soldiers were willing to risk their lives in defense of democracy thousands of miles from their home.

Obviously, I could never say I am thankful that the war in Vietnam happened. How could anyone be thankful for an event that killed more than four million Asians and almost sixty thousand Americans? Who could find satisfaction in a war that divided countries, wrecked millions of lives, and produced so much anguish with so little gained?

Not me. But I do believe good can surface from evil and triumph can emerge from tragedy. The conflict in Vietnam was catastrophic on many levels. But some good things—and many great people—have risen from the ruins of a war-torn Vietnam. Two of those great people are my parents, Ho and Tammy (Tam) Nguyen. To me, they are the true embodiment of the American dream, and they are truly my heroes. If there were any victors in the aftermath of the war in Vietnam, it was people like my parents. Their victory was gained not by defeating someone but rather by surviving the ordeal and thriving when a new opportunity was granted to them.

They don't claim a victory, and they certainly didn't ask for the war in Vietnam. They weren't political activists, they weren't warmongers, and, for the most part, they weren't particularly interested in the fight against the North Vietnamese Army or the Vietcong. People like my parents simply wanted peace. Their focus in life was on serving God and providing for their family. They did not completely understand the conflict; they did not embrace the battle. For them, the war was more of a circumstance to avoid than a cause to die for. That may seem extremely unpatriotic to Americans, who have been raised and trained to defend the United States, to celebrate the Fourth of July, to protect the Constitution, and to be willing to die for all that the United States of America represents. I feel that way about America. But I don't think you can compare Vietnam to the United States in many ways, especially patriotism.

Vietnam literally means Land of the South, but based on its bloody and tumultuous history, it could easily be known as the Land of the Sword. The battles and wars in Vietnam date back to 200 BC, and for much of the last century, machine guns have been as much a part of the landscape as conical hats in the rice fields. By the late 1960s, many people in Vietnam were simply nauseated by the constant conflicts. Even many adults in the South had been taught as children that Ho Chi Minh was a great patriot of the entire region. Ho had that reputation until the mid-1940s, which would help explain why a villager in the South might be willing to hide a killer from the North.

Confusion, strife, and overall war-weariness all played a role in my grandparents' settling along the coastline of South Vietnam in Ben Da, a relatively small village of some nine thousand to ten thousand people. As the crow flies, Ben Da was about fifty-five to sixty kilometers south of Saigon, which is now Ho Chi Minh City. Vietnam's coastline borders the South China Sea in a shape that resembles an S. A majority of the strategic battles were located at the midway point of the S—at or near the Demilitarized Zone (DMZ). But Ben Da was much closer to the tail end of the S, tucked away along a small harbor near the Mekong Delta. In Ben Da, my family was approximately 650 kilometers from combat hot spots such as Da Nang.

Living in Ben Da didn't mean my family—I have three sisters and two brothers—was oblivious to the war, but the town was far enough away from the day-to-day combat that most of the time they could put the bloodshed out of their minds. The image many Americans have of a child in Vietnam is of Kim Phuc, the screaming, nine-year-old girl running naked down a road after a misplaced napalm strike on her village in South Vietnam. That photo remains a lasting image of the Vietnam conflict, but fortunately for my family—particularly my five older siblings—that was not the type of thing that happened in Ben Da.

In Ben Da in the early 1970s, my older brothers and sisters ran through the streets, hiked on the trails, played along the coastline, and lived a mostly carefree existence. My oldest brother, Ho, was ten at the time my family escaped from Vietnam in 1975. He remembers hearing about the war, but he never experienced any of the mayhem linked to it. He remembers thinking, even at eight or nine, that if things continued as they were, he would be required to join the war effort in six or seven years. But to a child, that seemed like forever. And to all of my siblings, the battlefields and carnage seemed like something that would never reach them. They had a sense of security and were able to enjoy, for the most part, the innocence of youth. That's what my father wanted for his kids, and that's why he worked so hard.

Describing my father's work ethic is difficult. He's James Brown—the hardest working man in show business—without the rhythm. He possesses Richard Simmons's energy, and the two are actually about the same height. And when it comes to work, the man is a machine. My dad, who was also raised in Ben Da, had his first job at eleven, walking five to six miles to the next village with bamboo shoots on his back. He'd sell his "cargo" and return to his home that afternoon or evening (he'd stay as long as it took because he didn't want to carry the shoots back). Upon arriving home, he would lay his profits on my grandparents' table and go to bed. That was his routine five days a week, and on the weekends he would attend school at the Catholic church in Ben Da. The priests would teach my father and the other children in the village how to read and write, and afterward, my grandfather would teach him how to shrimp and build the strongest nets in South Vietnam.

Obviously, my father didn't have much free time, and he certainly didn't waste any money; he learned at a very early age the value of both time and money. Because of his work ethic, my family was considered wealthy, at least by Vietnamese standards, in the early 1970s. My father was somewhat like the Sam Walton of Ben Da, a mover and shaker who made the most of every opportunity. He had worked the shrimp boats as a teenager until he and my mother could buy their own house. It was built on a big, brick box with water underneath. The water served dual purposes: it was my family's drinking water, and it also cooled the home during the blistering summers. You could almost say there were only two seasons in Vietnam. The summers were miserable, with temperatures at 100 degrees or more and humidity usually ranging from about 99 to 100 percent. Quite a range, huh? In other words, it was much like Houston without air conditioning. But the water directly underneath my parents' home did serve as a primitive air conditioner. And the house was solid enough to protect my family from the other season in Vietnam: the monsoon months. Beginning in September and extending through February and into March, the rain didn't just fall, it poured vertical and even horizontal sheets.

My brothers and sisters remember their home in Ben Da as being massive. It really wasn't particularly big, one of my cousins informed me when he returned to Vietnam several years ago. But it was much bigger than many of the other dwellings in Ben Da. It actually resembled a hotel of sorts, with dividing walls separating my family from other families. So it was pretty important to like your neighbors, because they were just a thin wall away. By Western standards, it certainly wasn't a dream home, but it was upscale for Ben Da. As my mother and father began filling up their home with children, my dad worked harder and harder. He worked the shrimp boats from before dawn until after dusk and finally saved enough money to put his career on solid footing. Literally. He left the boats behind and opened his own marine supply store, which he operated out of the back of the house.

(I told you earlier how much he valued time. Running a business in the back of your home really cuts down on commuting time.)

My father also understood customer service, and after some early struggles, he had pretty much cornered the market in Ben Da. He made it a point to know his customers by name, to provide reliable services and products, and to go to whatever lengths necessary to be successful. In fact, he was so successful that my oldest brother, Ho, was able to steal as much as a hundred dollars a day from my father's wallet. My dad was bringing in so much money that he never even missed it. "If there had been no war, I think Dad would have become a millionaire," my brother told me. "I know it. His business was a big success. From the other kids I knew in Vietnam, I knew we had plenty of money. I used to steal money from his pockets every day until Mama caught me one day and punished me. To this day, I hate even the thought of stealing. I learned my lesson that day, but I'm convinced that if we had not had a war, he would have become a millionaire."

He never reached that income level in Vietnam, but he was successful enough to buy a Jeep, which in that day and place was the equivalent of having a house with a three-car garage, backyard swimming pool, and cobblestone driveway in the United States. Among other things, my dad used the Jeep to drive to Saigon to stock up on marine supplies. And once he was in the bustling metropolis of approximately eight million people, he also kept close tabs on what was happening on the war front. He never let my siblings worry that major troubles were looming, but he knew that eventually he might need an escape plan. He saved his money, accumulated pieces of gold, and bought a radio so he could distinguish the real information from the propaganda. And, while he hoped and prayed his family would never come face-to-face with the war, he continually prepared for the worst-case scenario. Thank God he did. If he hadn't, the story of my family could very easily have ended on the night of April 28, 1975.

CHAPTER 3
Flee for All

BY **EARLY JANUARY** in 1975, the news coming across my father's four-band radio was not good. Despite a cease-fire that had been signed in Paris two years earlier, the North Vietnamese Army (NVA) launched a major offensive on January 6, capturing Phuoc Long City and the surrounding province. On March 1, an even more powerful offensive was unleashed on the Central Highlands of South Vietnam, resulting in nearly sixty thousand troops dead, injured, or missing. By March 25, 1975, Hue, the third largest city in South Vietnam, and the Quang Tri province had fallen to the Communist regime. It was clear to everyone that the outcome of this war was no longer in question. South Vietnam would soon fall, and all the freedoms we had enjoyed would cease to exist.

My father was well aware of this fact, and he had begun serious preparations for a family escape plan early in 1975. But it was essential for him to be extremely cautious in making his plans and even more guarded in whom he trusted. South Vietnam was filled with spies who would quickly and willingly provide information—escape plans, military initiatives, troop locations, and the political preferences of the residents—to the enemy to gain favor with the NVA. As the NVA and Vietcong moved farther and farther south, these traitors were responsible for the brutal slayings of thousands of innocent men, women, and children. With each village and town that fell, the NVA would quickly determine which residents fell into the category of "Traitor to the People's Cause." If you had served in the South Vietnamese Army, aided its soldiers, spoken out against the NVA, planned to escape the country, or anything else deemed to be detrimental to the Communist movement, you and your family were subject to severe public beatings, imprisonment, torture, or even summary execution. Quite often, all it took to be proven guilty of such "crimes" was the accusation of a snitch.

So, my father went about his evacuation plans in as much secrecy as possible. In addition to following the progress of the war on his radio, he heard the stories of the unmerciful NVA slayings from hundreds of South Vietnamese refugees who had been driven out of their homes as the war front moved south. By April of 1975, the once-quiet, relatively small community of Ben Da was overflowing with homeless victims of the war. The small Catholic church in Ben Da served as the initial shelter for the refugees, and once the church filled to its capacity, the migrating masses camped outside the church, in the streets, and wherever else they could find. In early April, Ben Da had turned into a tent city of sorts as the NVA had taken control of twelve provinces and more than eight million people. Finally, on April 28, 1975, the war that once seemed so far away from my siblings arrived on our back porch.

It was time to put my father's plans into action. My siblings went to bed that evening just as they had done on virtually every other night of their lives—with few fears, concerns, or worries.

But as darkness fell, my mother, who was four months pregnant with me at the time, hurriedly and frantically awoke my two brothers and three sisters. My father had received the word from his associates that it was time to go, and there wasn't a minute to waste. The NVA was on the move, and by morning, Ben Da would become like the rest of South Vietnam: under the oppression of the Communist movement. My parents were so intent on leaving as soon as they received the word that they didn't even bother changing my siblings out of their pajamas. They herded up the kids, grabbed a few clothes and a handful of possessions, and left their home that night, knowing they would never return. They had no idea where they would end up or how it would all turn out. But my father was brave enough to risk the lives of his family members so that we could pursue the life he believed we deserved. Sometimes courage is about standing your ground. But in this particular case, my father's courage was defined by his willingness to flee.

My parents had decided that they would rather die seeking freedom than raise their children in a culture of oppression, denigration, and religious persecution. Freedom means different things to different people, but to my parents, its most important element was the freedom to worship as they chose. My mother and father willingly and faithfully went to their knees in prayer, but they were not willing to bow to Communism, Buddhism, Ho Chi Minh, or any mortal man. They realized that in attempting to escape they might watch their children be slain by gunfire. But for them, it was better than exposing them to a life of brainwashing propaganda. It's been said that Communism is the death of the soul. So it was primarily with our souls in mind that my parents and siblings left their home for the final time in Ben Da on April 28.

My father had heard several believable rumors that a large ship would be waiting for refugees beyond the Saigon River in the South China Sea. His initial plan was to pay for a smaller boat to take our family into safer international waters where we could board an oil tanker or ocean liner. My father didn't own a boat, but he knew plenty of fishermen who trusted him and valued him as a friend because of the way he had treated them while conducting business in his marine supply store. Dad struck a deal with one of those fishermen, paying him with pieces of gold, and the fisherman agreed to take our family and five other families into international waters. So, on my family's final night on Vietnamese soil, my father, mother, and siblings began a five-mile hike through wooded areas and along the coastline to the fishing boat that would hopefully carry us to a larger vessel. I've tried to visualize this particular scene in my own mind many times. Here's my diminutive father leading my pregnant mother and five small children on a five-mile march for their lives, hoping to avoid detection by the NVA or traitors of the South and praying first to catch the fishing boat and then to make connections with a Mayflower-like vessel. My oldest brother, Ho, was only ten at the time, and my youngest brother, Hung, was no more than an infant. People occasionally ask me why I am not a worrier and seem to take things in stride. That image of my family is certainly one of the reasons I've rarely allowed day-to-day hassles or minor issues to bother me.

We were, indeed, delivered out of that situation, although not exactly as my father had planned. My family finally reached the fishing boat, which was stocked with a minimal amount of food and water. Approximately sixty people boarded the fishing boat that night, as my entire family stationed itself on one side of the boat along with another family. My siblings were still in their pajamas, and my parents gave their most valuable possession, the small four-band radio, to my oldest brother to keep it hidden from the others. My mother figured that if anyone already on the boat or anyone who boarded it later was going to steal valuables from others, they would first check the adults and might bypass the children. So, for the duration of my family's stay on that boat, Ho either clung to the radio or kept it out of sight.

Two other families positioned themselves on the other side of the fishing boat, and another family moved to the front, while a sixth family set up a makeshift camp toward the back of the boat. The fishing boat did feature a cabin, but that was reserved only for the captain and his family. Everybody else was treated to outdoor accommodations on the hard, wooden deck with a crystal clear view of the stars, the water . . . and the machine gun fire that would soon begin. As our boat ventured away from land and into the South China Sea, my family joined numerous other boats that floated away from the shore in anticipation of a large rescue vessel. We were still relatively close to land—only half a mile or so away from shore—when the machine gun fire and bombs began turning the calm waters into what became a watery grave for many refugees. The NVA was attempting to prevent a mass exodus, and the assorted motor boats, fishing boats, canoes, and rafts were the targets of the bombings. Several of my siblings can vividly recall the explosions and the splashes of gunfire as we attempted to make our escape. The NVA and Vietcong were intent on teaching the would-be escapees a lesson. The North government's leaders viewed the fleeing refugees as prospective laborers and glorified slaves, who would carry out the tedious and sometimes torturous chores of a Communist workforce. And in the Communist way of thinking, it was better to kill the refugees than to allow them to escape their future responsibilities in building a new empire.

As our motorized fishing boat powered farther and farther away from the shore, my family members recognized that we were one of the lucky refugee boats. We would be able to elude the barrage of bullets and bombs that took the lives of many others who had been in a holding pattern with us only moments earlier. But as we moved farther away from land over the next day, it also became apparent that the big boat we had hoped to connect with was already gone. We were completely on our own. Ship out of luck, so to speak.

As it turned out, we may have been lucky that there wasn't an oil tanker around. I've read the stories of other Vietnamese boat people who watched in horror as their family members and friends tried to board five-story vessels from smaller boats. The people already on board the tanker would toss down a rope and hope that the refugees on the smaller boats were strong enough to pull themselves up to safety. If they weren't, they would often fall to their death, drowning in the sea or cracking their heads against the smaller boats underneath them. I have a difficult time imagining my pregnant mother climbing that rope by herself—let alone with my youngest brother in one arm. And I can't really picture my young sisters climbing that rope, either. But I do know my father would have died trying to get them up the rope and onto the boat. Perhaps it was fortunate for us all that the large vessel was never an option. My family never saw one, and all on board resigned themselves to the reality that the fishing boat was their only hope for safety.

Our captain made a decision to take the fishing boat south around the far southern tip of Vietnam and then to sail northwest into the Gulf of Thailand. We would then sail beyond the Cambodian shoreline, where Khmer Rouge soldiers, aided by the NVA and Vietcong troops, had overthrown the Cambodian government. Our captain's goal was to find refuge in Thailand. With a relatively small boat, it was a less risky journey than attempting to travel northeast to Hong Kong, where Queen Elizabeth of England had granted refugees a temporary safe harbor. But the much shorter trip to Thailand also came with a tremendous risk. Thai pirates developed a notoriously vicious and barbaric reputation for attacking refugee boats, boarding the ships, killing the men, raping the women, and stealing everything of value. There are hundreds of gruesome tales about these Thai pirates, who would sometimes kill the men, beating them to death with clubs, oars, and hammers. Other times, the pirates would force the men at gun point to watch as they raped their wives, daughters, sisters, and mothers and then threw the women overboard. But with a limited supply of fresh water, the captain decided it was a risk he would need to take. After all, there was certainly no option of turning back.

On April 29, U.S. Marines and Air Force helicopters, flying from carriers offshore, began a massive airlift. In a span of some eighteen hours, more than one thousand American civilians and almost seven thousand Vietnamese refugees were flown out of Saigon. At 4:03 a.m. on April 30, two U.S. Marines were killed in a rocket attack at Saigon's Tan Son Nhut Airport. They were the last reported Americans to die in the Vietnam war effort. At dawn, the last Marines of the force guarding the U.S. embassy lifted off, and only hours later, looters ransacked the embassy while North Vietnamese tanks rolled into Saigon, ending the war. In fifteen years, nearly one million NVA and Vietcong troops and a quarter of a million South Vietnamese soldiers had died. Hundreds of thousands of civilians had also been killed. But despite all the efforts to prevent it from happening, Vietnam was now completely under the control of Ho Chi Minh and the Communist regime.

The Vietnam my parents had once known and loved was gone. Of course, there wasn't any point in lamenting what had been lost. What mattered most now was to be found by the right people. Everyone on board our boat still held out hope that we would be found by a friendly, freedom-loving vessel. Along with the horrifying stories of the pirates, there are also numerous stories of Vietnam boat people who were rescued by ships from the United States, England, and other democratic countries. But for us, those hopes never were realized. So, for approximately one month, the sixty or so people on the boat did as little as possible in order to conserve energy and cut down on the need for water consumption. Food was not much of an issue. We were on a fishing boat, after all. But as the ship made its way to Thailand, the need for drinking water was a major concern.

So was the weather. My brother recalls several very rough days on the sea. On those days, the families on the deck of the boat would huddle together and wrap their arms around each other. It was beyond motion sickness, as all my siblings swallowed hard to prevent from throwing up and further risking dehydration. But most often, that was a losing battle. As the waves crashed against the boat and poured onto the huddled families on the deck, my mother prayed vigilantly for the safety of all her children, including the one in her womb. Under normal circumstances, being four months pregnant would mean that she was past the point where most miscarriages occur. But these were certainly not normal circumstances. With rationed supplies of water, no medical care, and storms occasionally pounding our boat, the pregnancy was still at risk. For that matter, even going to the bathroom was a risky endeavor. The bathroom facilities were little more than a hole that opened up into the ocean. You sat above the hole and looked down into the ocean. You could see the propeller of the fishing boat, and my mother constantly warned my siblings that if they slipped into the hole they would be gone forever.

Fortunately, that never happened. And fortunately for everyone on that fishing boat, we arrived in a Thai port in late May—some thirty days after leaving Vietnam. Of course, making it to Thailand was only half the battle.

Thailand was an ally of the United States throughout the conflict in Vietnam. In fact, the U.S.-Thai security cooperation stemmed from a 1962 arrangement that obligated the United

States to come to Thailand's aid if it was attacked. And during the Vietnam conflict, Thailand allowed the United States to stage air attacks from Thai bases. So the government in Thailand was at least sensitive to the needs of the initial waves of refugees that landed in the country's ports and on its shores in the spring of 1975. But despite the fact Thailand had received $2 billion in U.S. economic and military aid since 1950, the country was not in any economic position to begin accepting thousands of homeless, jobless, and needy refugees as new citizens. All of the people on our fishing boat, as well as many others who arrived from South Vietnam on other boats, were forced to remain on board as the paperwork process began to unfold. In other words, we were welcomed in the port, but we were not permitted to set foot on solid ground.

But here again, we were extremely lucky. As the war in Vietnam ended, much of the free world opened its arms to the refugees who escaped from the Communists. The refugees arriving in 1975 were quickly resettled in other countries, such as the United States, France, Canada, Australia, the United Kingdom, Denmark, Austria, Italy, and West Germany. Many of the refugees who arrived in later years were not so lucky.

By late 1975, the flow of refugees out of Vietnam had slowed, as the Communist regime promised safety and security for all the people because Vietnam was now unified. But according to many documented accounts, those promises went unfulfilled. Fortunately, many of my extended family members also successfully escaped Vietnam. But family friends who were left behind continued to watch helplessly as life in Vietnam grew worse by the day as the Communist government took complete control. The residents of the former Republic of South Vietnam were initially forced to turn in all their money in exchange for a new currency. That process was intended to eliminate any wealth in the South, and everyone received an equal, paltry amount of the new currency. The working climate and the general morale of the citizens continued to decline in the years following the end of the fighting.

From 1978 to 1981, thousands and thousands of refugees attempted to escape on overcrowded and rickety boats. But even if they made it to another country, the trials were often just beginning. At one point, Hong Kong began refusing to accept any more refugees and forced some boats back to sea after supplying them with food and water. In desperation, some refugees sank their own boats at night in order to pressure the local authorities to accept them. Others were forced to remain on board the boats for several months before they were allowed to disembark. And some spent years in refugee camps that were overcrowded, understocked, and served as little more than prison camps. By 1989, the refugee situation was still so out of control and utterly hopeless in Thailand, Hong Kong, and other Asian countries that Vietnam agreed to take back the boat people without punishing them, as the United Nations High Commission for Refugees (UNHCR) monitored the "repatriation" program. According to the UNHCR, it wasn't until February of 2001 that the last Vietnamese boat people finally left Thailand, ending a saga that had lasted for more than a quarter of a century.

In comparison with those agonizingly long ordeals, my family's month-long stay in a Thailand port was practically a vacation. Although my family was not permitted to leave the port, the Thai government brought food and water every day to the fishing boat that became our floating motel. The living conditions still weren't ideal. My family was still sleeping on the deck and still exposed to the elements. But at least we were no longer exposed to gunfire or the potential raids of pirates. As my oldest brother recalls, perhaps the only real difficulty we were forced to deal with was the spicy Thai food the government delivered to us on a daily basis. According to Ho, the food was a mixture of fire and rice. Nevertheless, my family happily and thankfully accepted the generosity of the Thai government and continually prayed for the best-case relocation scenario. My parents didn't really care where we ended up. They were just extremely grateful to be out of a war-torn Vietnam and together as a family.

By late June—roughly two months after the harrowing escape from Ben Da on the night before the war came to an end—my parents received the official word that they were going to America. The paperwork had all been processed, and my family would soon be leaving Thailand to fly to California, where we would be temporarily located until we were sponsored by a church or some other organization. My parents and siblings had never been in an airplane, never spoken a word of English, and never before contemplated living in the U.S.A. But suddenly, my parents realized they had been granted a new lease on life. It was more than a bit scary for them, as they pondered all of the unknowns. But more than anything else, they felt blessed. My family boarded the plane for the United States with little more than their hopes, their dreams, each other, and that four-band radio that had proven so valuable in my father's evacuation plans.

We were coming to America—the home of the brave. And as I see it now, that was the ideal location for a man like my father. He had already proven his courage in leading his family out of harm's way. He would do the same once again as my family moved into a new era of our lives known as the American way.

CHAPTER 4
Born in the U.S.A.

I'VE PROBABLY BEEN ASKED hundreds—perhaps even thousands—of times, "What's the best thing about being a player in the National Football League?" Honestly, there are plenty of good things about being in the NFL, beginning with the economic opportunities. The average college student certainly doesn't come straight out of school and command a six-figure income. Obviously, the average college student doesn't put his career in jeopardy every time he goes to work, either. But I will never deny that the financial opportunities in the NFL are quite attractive for as long as they last. From the bottom of my heart, however, I absolutely promise you that money isn't my favorite thing about being a player in the NFL. My favorite thing about this lifestyle is, without question, being able to interact with the star-gazing kids who so often view NFL athletes as role models and heroes.

I love dealing with kids, working with kids, and being around kids. That's probably because I am still—and probably always will be—a kid at heart. Whenever I make a public appearance or do an autograph session, I sincerely try to engage each child I have the opportunity to meet. For the most part, the kids are genuine in their interest and usually excited to meet a player for the Dallas Cowboys. I'm sure some of the parents set their kids up to receive an autograph so they can make a buck or two on the signed memorabilia. But generally speaking, the kids just want a chance to meet me and have something signed so they can show their friends at school or in the neighborhood. Of course, there are always a handful of kids who come to an autograph session with absolutely no clue as to who I am. Their parents will tell them something like, "He plays for the Cowboys," or, "He's on TV," or, "He's a famous guy." These kids will typically saunter up to me without saying a word and hand me something to sign. I've seen guys who will simply sign the item and move on to the next person in line, but I like to try to have fun with everyone who bothers to stand in line to receive my autograph. And it's the kids who really don't know who I am that I'm likely to have the most fun with.

One of my favorite lines is, "Do you know who I am?" The kid will inevitably shake his head "no" as I reach out to shake his or her hand. Then, when the child is real close to me, I will smile and say, "I'm Jackie Chan." It usually draws a good laugh from the parents, as I provide a mock karate move. It's a joke, of course, and half the time, the youngsters don't know who Jackie Chan is, either. But Chan and I actually do have several things in common. We're both of Asian descent; we're both known for sacrificing our bodies for our professions; we both possess the physical scars to prove that we're a little bit crazy; and I suppose we can both trace our success in America to kicking on the West Coast. Chan was kicking on the big screen when he first arrived in Hollywood from Hong Kong, and I was kicking inside my mother's womb when my family first arrived at Camp Pendleton in California from Thailand.

We actually didn't spend much time in California, but that's where my family first officially set foot on American soil. I've also reminded my wife several times that, even though I was still in my mother's womb at the time, our limited stay in California is also probably where I got my rugged, Hollywood good looks. That's usually good for another boisterous laugh, as she reminds me that I have a mug tailor-made for a face mask.

California has long been a place where people with limited resources arrived with little more than their big dreams. That was certainly the case for my family, although my father wasn't looking for a place in show business—a job in any business would suit him fine. My siblings have told me that we were treated very well upon our arrival in the United States, and after a brief stay on the West Coast, we were bussed to Fort Chaffee in Arkansas, which is just east of the Oklahoma state border. A bus trip from California to Arkansas may sound like absolute misery to most of the population, but for my family, especially my siblings, it was like a free sight-seeing tour of their new country, filled with first-time views of U.S. landmarks such as the Arizona desert, the mountain ranges of New Mexico, and Stuckey's roadside travel stops. You can imagine their wide-eyed expressions as they gazed out the windows of that bus and came to the realization that they were, indeed, an awfully long way from Ben Da.

Once the bus finally arrived in Fort Chaffee in the summer of 1975, the fun was just beginning. Technically, it was a refugee camp, but to my siblings, it could easily have been labeled a summer youth camp. It was certainly a far cry from the tent city image many people have of refugee camps. Along with Camp Pendleton in California and Indiantown Gap in Pennsylvania, Fort Chaffee was one of the three largest refugee camps in the United States. In terms of where we were coming from and the overall accommodations, my family viewed Fort Chaffee as the Taj Mahal. "It was really nice," my oldest brother, Ho, still recalls.

"It was actually a lot more comfortable than where we lived in Vietnam."

It certainly featured plenty of amenities for the kids. My family lived in one of several multistory buildings on the base. For the most part, each family had its own room, so it was almost like a hotel, which added to the vacation feel. There were probably a hundred people in each of the buildings, but overcrowding wasn't a problem. And for the kids, it was like their own little world within a brand new world. All the Vietnamese kids in the refugee camp spent their days running around the base, playing hide-and-seek and sand volleyball and watching movies. There were some rather informal classes for the adults and older children to attempt to begin learning basic English, but for the most part, my siblings remember Fort Chaffee as Arkansas' Club Med.

By the end of the summer, my brothers and sisters were feeling quite at home at Fort Chaffee, which is located a few miles northeast of Fort Smith, Arkansas. Of course, by the end of the summer, my mother was feeling anything but comfortable for another reason. A pregnancy that began in Ben Da and continued in the South China Sea, Thailand, California, and on a cross-country bus trip was nearing delivery. I was born on September 25, 1975, in a setting that was far more sterile, safe, and technologically advanced than any of my brothers and sisters had been. It's not like they were born in a rice paddy, but the clinic in Ben Da where they were born could hardly compare to the hospital where I was born in Fort Chaffee, Arkansas. My mother and I received the best medical attention available, which may have had something to do with my eventual career as a middle linebacker in the National Football League.

I honestly don't know why I grew to be so much bigger than my parents or my older brothers. I've probably been questioned about that thousands of times by hundreds of reporters. Perhaps

I'm a genetic freak, although some of my friends have told me to leave out "genetic" and the description would fit better. But the more likely scenario is that I simply benefited from better nutrition than the rest of my family right from the start. My mother was actually given prenatal vitamin supplements when she arrived in the United States—something she did not receive in her other five pregnancies. And I was provided with nutrient-rich baby formula from an early age, which is also something my siblings never received. It's scientifically proven that you really are a product of what you eat, which would explain why I am nearly a foot taller and close to a hundred pounds heavier than my father was during his twenties.

During my infancy in Arkansas, I continued to receive outstanding medical care and formula, as the U.S. government officials continued to work on dispersing the families at the refugee camps throughout various regions of the country. Immigration agents in the United States had asked Congress to scatter the new immigrants across the country in order to prevent a ghetto effect among the refugee population. From the government's point of view, the key to placing a family was to find a suitable sponsor. Most of the Vietnamese families coming to the United States had no money, spoke no English, and knew very little—if anything—about the American culture. The sponsor, which in many cases was a church, took on the responsibility of not only helping with the necessities of life—food, housing, and some sort of income—but also helping with the painstaking process of adapting to a new way of life in a new country.

One of my father's sisters, whose family had also survived the escape from Vietnam and had spent some time in the Arkansas refugee camp, had been sponsored early in the fall of 1975 by a church in Michigan. So when a Catholic church in Kalamazoo, Michigan, was located as a potential sponsor, it made sense for our family to move north to begin a new life. When informed of this possibility, my parents were initially concerned about the cold weather. That had been the talk inside the refugee camp, and coming from the warm climate in South Vietnam, many of the refugees were worried about making a difficult adjustment even tougher by dealing with snow and ice. But when my dad contacted his sister by phone, she assured him that the weather was fine. She said something like, "Don't worry about the weather. It's wonderful. Come on up; you'll love it."

Of course, that was in early fall, when the weather in Michigan is usually close to ideal. But by the time we were actually sponsored, it was December, and the weather then may be ideal for refugees from Antarctica, but not for those from South Vietnam. Nevertheless, we arrived at the Catholic church in Kalamazoo at about the same time a major snowstorm did. It was the first time anyone in my immediate family had ever seen snow, which initially created some excitement. But the newness quickly wore off, as my parents and siblings realized that the best kind of weather was the kind that didn't need to be shoveled. The brutally cold temperatures, along with the ice and snow, made for a miserable time in Michigan. My mother even had a fairly serious fall on the icy sidewalks, which expedited my father's resolve to move his family into a warmer climate.

It's a shame the weather was such a shock and such a source of misery to my family, because aside from the cold, our stay in Kalamazoo was actually an extremely positive experience. The eight of us came to Michigan with virtually nothing. But the priests and parishioners of the Catholic church that sponsored us catered to our every need. First of all, they set us up with a cozy house that was completely furnished, including items such as pots, pans, toiletries, towels, and everything else we needed. The house was even stocked with a refrigerator full of food when we first arrived. Every week, church members would take my parents to the grocery store to help them shop and find their way around. My father worked inside the church as a handyman and janitor, while my mother cared for me and my older siblings attended American public schools. My father fit right in, working hard in the church and impressing our sponsors with his dedication and meticulous attention to detail. He didn't understand the language, but he certainly understood what it took to make a living and a positive impression.

My school-age brothers and sisters, however, didn't experience such a smooth transition. Ho, for example, was eleven when we arrived in Kalamazoo. He was exceptional in math, but since he didn't know any English, he went to school with the kindergartners. Imagine how awkward an eleven-year-old would feel in a room full of five- and six-year-olds, especially since the younger kids were so much further advanced than he in terms of their English vocabulary skills. Ho was old enough to babysit his classmates, but initially he wasn't able to communicate with them or his teacher. But I will say this for my oldest brother: He was definitely the toughest kid in kindergarten. None of those five-year-olds ever once pushed him around.

As my siblings struggled with the language barrier and attempted to fit in at school, my father continued to work hard at the church. But with each blizzard and each cautious step on the frozen concrete, he longed for a warmer climate. In the subfreezing temperatures of Michigan, he was simply a fisherman out of water. So, as he worked and provided for his family, my dad saved every penny he could, making plans to leave Michigan eventually. With his own funds and the help of the church parishioners, he bought a gas-guzzling dinosaur of a car—a 1969 Ford LTD—for five hundred dollars. And six months after arriving in Kalamazoo, my mom and dad loaded all six of us into the LTD and began another cross-country journey to Fort Worth, Texas, where some other relatives had settled. Here again, I have this vivid image of the Vietnamese version of the Griswolds, loading up the family car with everything we own in a cross-country misadventure.

My father, after all, couldn't even read any road signs and couldn't read the map. Ho, with his kindergarten English education, was the navigator for the trip, deciphering a six-page map that took us from Kalamazoo to Cowtown. Fortunately, we didn't have a wreck. None of us wore seat belts—remember it was 1976—and we certainly didn't have a car seat for me. My parents and siblings took turns holding me, while my youngest brother traveled most of the trip lying across the monstrous back dash, with his face plastered against the back window. I think of the safety precautions we now take in buckling up our children in the backseat and wonder how any of us lived through our childhood.

Nonetheless, my family made it to Fort Worth reasonably sane and relatively unscathed. My father immediately got a job doing industrial jobs, warehouse work, and anything else that would put food on the table, as the rest of the family attempted to make things work in the crowded conditions of my uncle's home. Here again, though, my mother and father didn't feel at home. The weather was warmer, but my father had spent his entire life living just a stone's throw away from the South China Sea, and he was longing to be back near the water. So, four months after arriving in Fort Worth, we loaded up the LTD again and went to join other relatives in New Orleans.

The Big Easy wasn't necessarily a big hit with my family, although we stayed in New Orleans for almost two years. I don't remember anything about the city, but that's when my parents both began working around the clock. Both my mother and father took various jobs, and they were almost never at home. My dad found some manual labor jobs, at which he made seven or eight dollars an hour, which was pretty good money at the time, and my mother would be up before dawn working in various roles. Ho was left in charge of the rest of us, although he would often hop the fence to go play cards for long periods at our cousin's house. He would return just long enough to cook us lunch and dinner, which most often consisted of boiled hot dogs and potato chips. After two years in New Orleans, we continued our nomad ways, moving to Biloxi, Mississippi. My father returned to his comfort zone and began shrimping in Biloxi. He bought a twenty-eight-foot boat, which was tiny in comparison with most of the shrimping boats in the Gulf, and he worked incredibly hard. At the end of each day, his hands were calloused, and his back was throbbing because he had to pull the nets in by himself. Nowadays, the shrimp nets are attached to a pulley system that can be reeled in rather effortlessly. But back then, my father did it all by hand. Despite the long, brutal days, he generally felt more comfortable living on the banks of the Gulf of Mexico and making his living in the water. But when he heard about a thriving hotspot for shrimpers on the coast of Texas, he knew instantly that it was a sign from above.

Loosely translated, the Vietnam village we came from, Ben Da, means, "port of rocks." When my parents heard that the shrimping was especially good in a Texas town called Rockport, they took it as an omen and an answer to their prayers. Almost immediately, my dad loaded his boat onto a trailer and loaded the kids back into the family car. For the fifth time since we had been sponsored by the church in Kalamazoo, the Nguyen family was on the move again. But this time, there was a genuine belief inside our car that we were going to a place that seemed destined to be our home. On the trip from Mississippi to Rockport, my mother probably led the family in ten to twelve prayers. That's not an uncommon practice in any car where my mother is a passenger. Throughout my childhood, I remember that any trip in the car that lasted up to an hour usually featured at least twenty to twenty-five minutes of prayer. My mother always carried the

Catholic Rosary with her, and we would typically recite the entire Rosary. We didn't need a radio; we had the traveling Tammy Nguyen praise and worship show that never lost its signal. My mother always prays with a purpose, but on that trip she was especially resolute. She longed for a place to plant family roots, and based on everything my parents had heard and were feeling, Rockport-Fulton seemed like a place they could truly call home.

In addition to its location on the banks of Aransas Bay and its reputation as a shrimper's haven, Rockport-Fulton had, at that time, become a destination for at least one hundred families of former Vietnam refugees. Philosophically, I understand the original intent of U.S. immigration officials in dispersing the refugees throughout the country, but as time went by, many of those former residents of Vietnam migrated back to settings that seemed much more like their native home and to communities where they found relatives and others who shared their culture and language. And in many cases, that meant being close to the ocean. Several of my extended relatives had already discovered Rockport-Fulton, and when our family arrived along the Texas coast, we experienced a comfort level that we had not found in any of our other stops in the United States.

My father immediately put his small boat in the waters of the Aransas Bay and went to work. He was determined to make sure this would be our final move. Money was extremely scarce at first, and all eight of us lived in a tiny room at a motel called the Offshore Inn. It wasn't actually government housing, but it was very inexpensive, and many of the rooms at the Offshore Inn were occupied by Vietnamese refugees. My parents worked extremely hard, saving every penny they could. My mom would be up at 4:00 a.m. shucking oysters for a local restaurant before beginning her full-time job at the Sand Dollar Pavilion, where she washed dishes and cleaned tables. Meanwhile, my dad was laboring in his boat from sunup to sundown. Occasionally, at the end of a long day, my father and a friend would share a beer after they had sold their haul for the day. But literally, they would share one beer. We didn't have enough money for each of them to have his own beer.

As my parents slaved, they also saved. My father watched as the bigger shrimp boats sailed into the Gulf and brought back hauls that were twice the size of his. He analyzed the potential lost wages and decided to build his own boat. He had had some carpenter training as a young boy in Ben Da, but he had never built a boat. Nevertheless, he took the money he had been saving and purchased the materials to build a larger boat. He and my uncle would shrimp during the day and work into the wee hours of the morning building that boat. I don't know if he ever really slept, and to this day, I am amazed at his resolve. Several months after beginning the project, he was able to sell that twenty-eight-foot boat and set sail in his new, forty-seven-foot boat, which enabled him practically to double his daily income. With the extra income, my family moved into the first house where we lived in Rockport. We moved out of the Offshore Inn, and we were all grateful to be in a place to call our own. My father would later build a house for my grandfather, who also settled in Rockport, and then built the house where my parents still live in just nineteen days.

By all accounts, living in Rockport-Fulton was, indeed, working out better for us than anyone in my family had really ever anticipated. We had extended family members surrounding us; we were making a living and doing more than merely making ends meet; and we were feeling more at home than we had at any other place in the United States. For a short time, it seemed as though we had found an oasis where things couldn't get any better. Little did we know that things were about to take a turn for the worse.

In Rockport, we didn't detect the same warm, welcoming feelings my family had initially experienced in Michigan and had later found in other parts of the country. After all, many of the longtime residents of Rockport, as well as many other communities along the Texas Gulf Coast, felt economically threatened by the migrating masses of Vietnamese refugees who were suddenly seeking to make a living on the same waters that Americans once dominated. The U.S. shrimpers had their routine, and they were certainly not thrilled when Vietnamese families pooled their money together and began filling up those waters—from Galveston to Corpus Christi—with shrimp boats. Furthermore, the Vietnamese fishermen were literally hungrier than the majority of the established white fishermen. With little or no money in their pockets, the Vietnamese shrimpers were willing to get up earlier and stay out later than many of the American shrimpers, who already owned homes and refrigerators filled with food. But the Vietnamese fishermen knew that their families' next meal often depended on what they did that day. The Vietnamese fishermen would sometimes put their entire families in a boat, and they often worked from dawn to long past dusk seven days a week, celebrating if they turned a profit of more than ten to fifteen dollars a day. As a result, the Vietnamese shrimpers began seriously cutting into the profits of the longtime residents of the Texas coastline, reducing the available catch and keeping wholesale prices low.

My father doesn't talk much about those times, and I was too young to remember the specific events. But according to some of my family members' accounts and an excellent article written by University of North Carolina law professor Andrew Chin ("The KKK and the Vietnamese Fishermen," available on the web at www.unclaw.com/chin/scholarship/fishermen.htm), the white fishermen initially attempted to ward off the Vietnamese by gouging them for the prices they charged for boats and supplies. The Americans also pressured the owners of local bait shops, marine supply stores, and seafood retailers and wholesalers not to do business with the Vietnamese shrimpers. They also lobbied the Texas legislature for stiffer restrictions and higher costs on new shrimp boat licenses. But when none of those things seemed to deter the refugees, things turned ugly. Several Vietnamese-owned shrimp boats were burned along the coast from 1979 to 1981, and arson investigators later determined that the fires had been intentionally set. Several Vietnamese shrimpers reported sniper fire while at sea, and on August 3, 1979, several Vietnamese boats were burned and a vacant home owned by a Vietnamese family was firebombed in Seadrift, Texas, which is about forty miles northeast of Rockport along the San Antonio Bay. On that same night, a fight broke out between Vietnamese and white fishermen, resulting in the fatal shooting of a white crabber. Two Vietnamese men were later tried for murder and acquitted on grounds of self-defense.

The incident in Seadrift generated plenty of publicity and created even more distrust between the growing Asian population along the Texas coast and the longtime residents. Suddenly, our American dream seemed to be turning into a nightmare, which only escalated on Valentine's Day in 1981, when a group of white fishermen organized a rally that was attended by the Grand Dragon of the Texas Knights of the Ku Klux Klan and thirteen uniformed members of the Klan's military arm. According to published reports, Louis Beam, the Grand Dragon, told the white fishermen that he would give the government until the start of shrimping season in mid-May to remove the Vietnamese fishermen from the area. If that didn't happen, Beam said, he would call into action the Klan's 2,500-member Texas Emergency Reserve army and take matters into his own hands. During the rally, Beam demonstrated the best ways to burn a boat and was quoted in local newspapers as saying, "The Ku Klux Klan is more than willing to select out of the ranks of American fishermen some of your more hardy souls and send them through our training camps. And when you come out of that, they'll be ready for the Vietnamese."

Then in March of 1981, a group of armed, hooded Klansmen and Texas Emergency Reserve members conducted what they called a boat parade in the Gulf Coast waters. Along the way, they stopped to show off their weapons and make threats against the Vietnamese fishermen and their families on the docks and other boats. But perhaps the scariest threat of all was an effigy of a Vietnamese fisherman that hung from the rear deck.

By mid-April, Alabama civil rights attorney Morris Dees filed a wide-ranging lawsuit against the KKK, Beam, other specified Klansmen, and alleged unnamed conspirators in the federal district court for the Southern District of Texas. In essence, the Vietnamese fishermen were seeking a court order to prevent the KKK's threatened violence during the 1981 shrimping season, citing the Thirteenth and Fourteenth Amendments to the U.S. Constitution, and the common law of contracts and torts. Additionally, Dees claimed the Klan had violated two laws that have rarely been considered part of the civil rights arsenal: the 1890 Sherman Antitrust Act and an even older Texas statute prohibiting the operation of private armies.

As fate would have it, the judge assigned to the case was Gabrielle Kirk McDonald, who was the first African American in Texas and the third African American woman in the country to serve in the federal judiciary. When he learned that Judge McDonald was an African American, Beam referred to her in court as a "Negress" and asked her to disqualify herself because "her people" had a bias against the Klan. McDonald denied Beam's request and later said she received death threats and one-way tickets to Africa while she was presiding over the case. The four-day trial, which was covered by media throughout the state and around the nation, resulted in a court-issued preliminary injunction prohibiting the Klansmen from threatening, intimidating, or harassing the Vietnamese fishermen or inciting others to do likewise. The trial ended on May 14, one day before shrimping season began. And on May 15, U.S. marshals patrolled the seas in order to protect the Vietnamese fishermen, who worked all summer without incident. One year later—on June 9, 1982—the court issued a permanent injunction ordering the Texas Emergency Reserve to disband. The injunction also prohibited the Klan from maintaining military organizations, conducting military training, or parading in public with firearms.

That officially ended the saga. But unofficially, the Texas coast certainly wasn't singing in racial harmony. Even by 1985, when the movie *Alamo Bay* was released in theaters, plenty of racial unrest remained in Rockport and the surrounding areas. The movie, starring Ed Harris and Amy Madigan, portrayed the tense times along the Texas coastline from the perspective of an American Vietnam war veteran (Harris), who was in danger of losing his financial livelihood because of the refugee fishermen. The movie also featured—extremely briefly—an appearance by a Vietnamese kid dressed in some rather hideous, plaid pants. That kid was me. To be perfectly honest, I didn't even know at the time that the movie was about racial unrest. I was in second grade, and all I knew at the time was that it was a blast to miss six weeks of school toward the end of the year while we were filming. The producers of the film arranged for eight to ten of us to miss school during the production of the movie. My brother Hung and my sister LyLy, as well as my grandfather, were also in the movie as extras (the Ho Nguyen who was featured in the movie was not my brother). All the extras were paid fifty dollars a day to be in the movie, although I never saw any of the money because it went straight to my parents. The big perk for me for being in the movie was that I was able to eat free food—and lots of it—throughout the six weeks of filming.

It actually turned out to be a pretty good movie, although it received mixed reviews from the critics. I would recommend that you go rent it the next time you are at the local video store, but I have spent years trying to purchase every remaining copy so I will never again be teased and tormented about those ridiculous plaid pants. My big moment in the silver screen's spotlight came when a bunch of Vietnamese kids were playing softball. I caught the ball, tagged somebody out, and then the KKK arrived as we scattered. Looking back on it now, it's interesting to me that I appeared in the movie in a sports role. That was an ironic foreshadowing of how the racial unrest in Rockport would finally and fully come to an end years later. Of course, you may also find it ironic that another similarity between Jackie Chan and me is our movie credits. Now, please stop laughing and kindly turn the page.

CHAPTER 5

The Beauty of Sports

UNSUSPECTING FRIENDS fall for my antics almost every time I take them to my hometown for a stroll down memory lane or to eat at my parents' restaurant. I'll start building it up long before we approach the Rockport-Fulton area, and by the time we hit the Copano Bay Causeway, I can see the wheels spinning in their mind. When we cross the bay, I'll lay it on even thicker. "This billboard is steaming hot," I'll say. "It's sexy enough that it should probably be shrink-wrapped and behind the counter at the convenience store."

Inevitably, my male buddies will be eagerly looking for some suntan ad featuring a swimsuit model in a skimpy bikini. As we continue southbound on Texas State Highway 35, I'll hit them with everything I've got. "As soon as you see it, you'll be drooling," I say just before the billboard comes completely into focus. "Let me know if you want me to pull over so you can soak it all in. If you have a camera with you, pull it out." Once they see it—and once I see their stunned disappointment—I usually burst into laughter. Instead of tanned, toned beach beauties bathing in the sun, the billboard features something no one would ever want to see in a bikini: me. But at least it does show my mug in my best light: in a helmet.

Located just north of the Rockport and Fulton city limits near the tiny Aransas County Airport, the billboard is the first thing many visitors see when they enter the sister cities of Rockport and Fulton. I have fun joking about it with friends and family members, making light of the fact I'm the poster boy of the region. But in all sincerity, it does give me a tremendous amount of pride. I believe that the paper sign on a wooden billboard is a strong indication that miracles are possible. Though on a much smaller scale, the billboard with my picture on it is about like Rosa Parks's picture being featured on the "Welcome to Montgomery, Alabama" sign. My billboard, after all, is the welcome greeting for a community that was once filled with plenty of intense bitterness and some overt hatred toward "those gooks and slant-eyed chinks." At best, I was the black-headed, olive-skinned stepchild. But now, it's a community that welcomes thousands upon thousands of visitors—fishermen, tourists, and others—each year with a sign trumpeting me as its favorite son. "Welcome to Rockport-Fulton, Home of Dat Nguyen." I consider that message nothing short of miraculous.

A tropical storm could tear it up; a hurricane could knock it down; and, for that matter, an advertiser with deep pockets could purchase the space and cover it up. But none of those things can ever change the fact that it was there. That, in my opinion, is a stirring reminder of the awesome power and beauty of sports. The athletic world is full of problems. Open the sports page of your local newspaper on a typical day, and you may be bombarded with stories of greed, corruption, drugs, cheating, arrogance, and so forth. But at their pure core, the games we play are a beautiful thing. Playing sports truly helped to shape my

This photo of my parents is the only picture that made the trip from Vietnam to the United States. Nguyen family photo

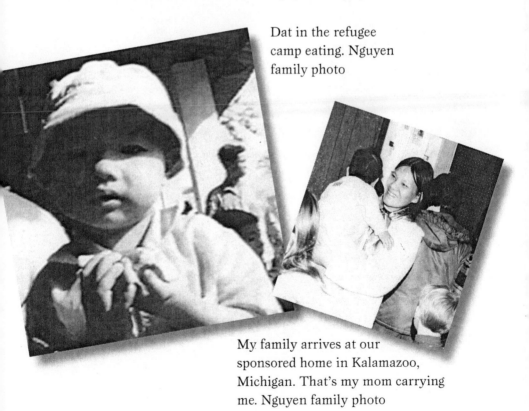

Dat in the refugee camp eating. Nguyen family photo

My family arrives at our sponsored home in Kalamazoo, Michigan. That's my mom carrying me. Nguyen family photo

My three sisters and my brother, Hung, pose for a quick snap shot. Nguyen family photo

Once my dad finished building this forty-seven-foot boat, he was practically able to double his daily haul of shrimp. Nguyen family photo

I sometimes joke with kids that I am Jackie Chan. I'm on the far right here, doing my best impersonation. Nguyen family photo

Young Dat.
Nguyen family photo

This photo was taken in junior high after I was the Offensive Player of the Game against Port Lavaca. I rushed for 134 yards and two scores. Nguyen family photo

My mother first opened a sandwich and coffee shop in 1993 just a stone's throw away from the water in Rockport, Texas. That sandwich shop became the now-famous Hu-Dat Restaurant. Photo by Rusty Burson

This is the first house we moved into after living in the Offshore Inn.
Photo by Rusty Burson

My dad built this home in Rockport in just nineteen days.
Photo by Rusty Burson

On Friday nights in the fall during
my senior season at Rockport-Fulton High School,
the crowds would be so big that fans would literally
line the fences. Photo by Rusty Burson

This is where my
sports career all
began—on the soccer
fields of Rockport-
Fulton. Photo by
Rusty Burson

I've been knocked around plenty of times since I played at Rockport-Fulton, but I can still remember the specific plays that helped unite a once-divided community. Photo by Rusty Burson

No matter where I go, I will always
be reminded that my roots are on shrimp
boats like these. Photo by Rusty Burson

life for the better. My coaches taught me lessons about discipline and perseverance I could never have learned in a classroom. Battling opponents on a field taught me about facing challenges in life. And perhaps most meaningful to me was what I witnessed happening in the stands of my hometown stadium. A team can unite a town, changing perceptions, prejudices, and people for the better. If you have ever seen the movie *Remember the Titans,* you know what I mean. When people become lost in the magic of following their team, the color of their jerseys becomes much more important than the color of their skin. That happened in *Remember the Titans.* It also happened in my hometown, where folks "Remember the Pirates."

People changed in Rockport-Fulton. Not all of them. Not overnight, either. But gradually, many people with preconceived notions and longstanding prejudices began to look at the Vietnamese immigrants and their families as neighbors instead of nuisances. Proudly, I believe I played at least a small role in some of the changes because of what I did on the fields and courts. I must admit, however, it was never my intention to be a civil rights activist or even to make a stand. I simply made a friend, and that one friendship put my life on a different course and eventually made a lasting impression on the community. Looking back, that friendship reminds me of a quote I once came across that states, "No problem is ever as dark when you have a friend to face it with you." I'm so thankful I had "Little Jimmy" Hattenbach with me to face the problems of my youth. As I recall, I got to know Jimmy's friendly face even before I really knew there were problems.

Because of the racial intolerance my parents had experienced and the overall hostile climate in the community, my parents warned my siblings and me to keep to ourselves at school. They didn't trust white people, and at the time, they figured it was in our best interest to adopt the same attitude. As time went by and tensions eased, my parents and other Vietnamese immigrants learned to trust their white neighbors and have made many friends among them. My instruction entering the first grade at Fulton Elementary School, however, was basically to rely on my siblings for help and to befriend only the other children of Vietnamese descent. My parents simply didn't know any better. They said the wrong things for what they perceived to be the right reasons. They believed they were doing the best thing to protect their children, and in their shoes in that climate, maybe I would have advised the same thing. But I was only six, and I was far more concerned about footraces than racial unrest. My vision of the big picture, at that point in my life, involved crayons and a Big Chief notepad. I didn't know how to sever racial ties; I barely knew how to tie my shoelaces.

My mother told me, "Dat, you're about to start school, and there are some things you need to know. It breaks my heart to tell you, but we can't trust the white people. We have to rely only on each other. You have to be cautious and learn to protect yourself. People will say mean things to you and not like you because of the color of your skin and where we came from. You should ignore them, you should stay away from them, you should not interact with them or cause any trouble." But this is what was actually running through my mind: "Dat, you're about to start school, and there are some things you need to know. They have a cafeteria with hot plate lunches and orange, push-up popsicles."

In other words, I wasn't particularly distrusting, cynical, or anything of the sort when a Caucasian kid named Jimmy Hattenbach said hello to me on our first day of first grade. When he greeted me, my mother's words and warnings were a thousand miles away. I looked at Jimmy, sized him up, and instinctively said the one thing that was most prominently on my mind: "Hey. Did you know they have orange, push-up popsicles in the cafeteria?"

From that point on, Jimmy and I were joined at the hip. We ate together, we played together, and, unknowingly, we soon made a major statement together. As we became friends, Jimmy asked me if I wanted to come over to his house to play after school. He didn't care that I was of Vietnamese descent, and perhaps most important, neither did his parents. Before he asked me to come over, Jimmy had discussed the matter with his parents, informing them that he had a new friend, but warning them that his friend was Vietnamese. His mother, Glenda, answered, "Jimmy, I don't care if your friend is Vietnamese, Chinese, Portuguese, black, white, green, or yellow. If he's your friend, he's welcome in our home." Considering the racial climate at the time, that statement alone was rather remarkable.

The Hattenbachs' house became more than a second home to me. At times in my youth and adolescence, it was my primary residence. When my parents moved to Corpus Christi during my freshman year in high school, I stayed in Rockport and lived with the Hattenbachs. Whenever I was tempted to believe the entire community was prejudiced against the Vietnamese, I looked toward the Hattenbachs. And when I needed anything, I often turned to the Hattenbachs. I often wonder how different my life would be today if Jimmy and I hadn't become such close friends so quickly. What if, for example, I had befriended someone else, gone over to his house, and been scorned by his parents because of my descent? Would I have been bitter and angry? Would I have believed my parents' warnings and withdrawn into the security of hanging out only with "my own kind?" Would I have played sports? Would that billboard of me ever have been on the outskirts of my hometown?

Who really knows? But I do believe Jimmy and I were drawn together by God for a higher purpose. Jimmy's father, Jimmy Sr., worked for the only seafood market in our community that, at the time, was willing to buy fish, shrimp, and shellfish from the

Vietnamese shrimpers. Casterline's Seafood Market enabled my father to make a living by allowing him to sell his daily haul. And seeing the dedication and work ethic of the Vietnamese shrimpers like my father, Jimmy Sr. had no reservations about letting his son invite a Vietnamese kid into his home. Jimmy Sr. also didn't have so much as a second thought about drafting me onto his youth soccer team. No other youth soccer coach in our community was willing to risk the possible scorn of the locals by drafting the son of a Vietnamese refugee onto his team, but Jimmy Sr. simply didn't care. He was already working for the only seafood market in town that would even deal with the Vietnamese fishermen, so he was already part of the scorned community. "I may have been on the so-called blacklist," Jimmy Sr. told me later, "but I was damn proud to be on it."

By drafting me onto his soccer team, he pretty much etched his name—at least at that time—into the blacklist hall of fame. But he didn't care, and I didn't have a clue. I didn't have any kind of political agenda for playing soccer; I just wanted to play for the love of the game, the thrill of the competition . . . and the halftime snacks. Remember, I was six. I primarily wanted to play because I thought it would be cool to have a uniform, and I really liked the idea of the snacks. If you have ever witnessed six-year-olds in youth soccer, you know that everything else—technique, strategy, fundamentals, and even winning or losing—takes a backseat to the halftime and postgame snacks. I suppose there were a handful of kids who actually knew what was going on and had some kind of sense for the game. I was definitely not part of that group. I eventually became a pretty good soccer player, but I was definitely not a natural.

I don't remember how we actually fared that first season. Nobody even officially kept score. But that was the start of my athletic career, and in some small way, it was the subtle beginning of a rather amazing transformation in our community. Beyond any doubt, I believe God was the driving force behind the gradual acceptance of the Vietnamese immigrants and their offspring in Rockport-Fulton. Plenty of people rolled their eyes when they first saw me out there on the soccer field playing with their kids. But in just a few years, we were raising eyebrows because we were beating their kids. By the time I was eleven, our fifteen-person soccer team had eleven Vietnamese players on the roster. Jimmy Hattenbach Sr. was still one of the only coaches in town willing to draft Vietnamese kids, and we made him look like a genius for his commitment to us. We played ten games that year and won all of them. Actually, we didn't just win; we were dominant. For the season, we outscored our ten opponents 67–4. At the end of the year when we accepted our league championship trophy in front of the rest of the teams and parents, nobody besides our own parents even clapped for us. And I mean nobody. They were making a loud statement about their resentment for the Vietnamese by sitting on their hands. But while they still may not have liked us, they had to respect us.

At least the people who cared about soccer respected us. Of course, there weren't too many people in my hometown—or my home state, for that matter—who really cared about soccer. Football was—and probably always will be—king in the Lone Star State. Even after we did so well in soccer, there was a sentiment in town that "the gooks may be good in soccer, but they'll never make it in a real sport like football." To be perfectly honest, I wasn't initially real keen on the idea of proving otherwise. When I left elementary school for Rockport-Fulton Junior High, I liked sports primarily because of the sense of belonging it gave me. Once I entered junior high, though, I discovered I could be part of a group without expending all the effort it took to be a part of a team. For lack of a better term, I hooked up with a gang. Not the kind of gang you see in the movies or on the news. We weren't organized, we didn't have colors, we didn't deal or do drugs, and I wouldn't have labeled us as a serious threat to society. Real gangs may be as mean as grizzly bears; we were more like gummy bears. But we did hang out together, and we were in training to become troublemakers. I smoked a few cigarettes, and to impress the older guys in my group, I stole a couple of car stereos and a few small items like chips or candy from convenience stores. Mainly, we just hung out on the streets and docks of Rockport and Fulton. We would ride our bikes, kick over trash cans, throw water balloons at cars, complain about everything under the sun, and try our best to be tough, rebellious, and, most of all, cool.

In reality, though, we were just dumb, bored, and, most of all, tired. I once stayed out of my house for two straight days and nights. Do you know how hard it is to stay up and be cool for forty-eight straight hours? Do you also realize how difficult it is to find something to do for two straight days? I discovered right away that being a rebellious punk was much harder than it looked. So I was already giving some serious consideration to hanging up my thugish ways as I dragged myself home after my two-day test drive as a full-time hooligan. I wouldn't say the streets of Rockport were particularly mean, but they weren't that friendly, either. If there was any lingering doubt in my mind about giving life as a hoodlum a little more time, those thoughts were washed away by what I discovered when I did go home. All of my clothes were stuffed into trash bags and were sitting on the front lawn. My parents told me I could be a punk if I wanted to, but they wanted no part of it and no part of me if that was how I chose to live my life. Besides, they were planning on moving to Corpus Christi eventually to start a new restaurant, and they didn't need the hassle of keeping up with a hoodlum son. At best, they threatened to send me to an all-male boarding school in Missouri. At worst, they threatened to let me see if I could make it on my own.

Shoot, I could barely make it on my own for two days. I wasn't about to push my luck any further. And the idea of going to an all-male boarding school made me sick at my empty stomach. I wasn't much of a ladies' man, but at least there was the possibility of lucking into a girlfriend if you were in a co-ed classroom. An all-male boarding school, on the other hand, brought to mind images of testosterone torture camp. I decided right then that it was time to turn over a new leaf. No more running with the wrong crowd; no more hanging out all night; no more stealing car stereos; and no more meals comprising a stolen bag of Doritos. I was going to keep my nose clean and my belly full. I was going to take school more seriously, and I was going to join a team. I was also going to choose my friends more wisely, which led me right back to Jimmy Hattenbach.

While I was sowing my junior high "wild oats," Little Jimmy was playing football at Rockport-Fulton Junior High, and he was a pretty good player. Aside from tossing the pigskin around from time to time and tackling my brothers or cousins in a front-yard game, I never really had a burning desire to hit the gridiron. I fell in love with basketball in eighth grade, and I believed I had found my niche. My father was about five-foot-nothing, and my mother was four-foot-something. But for whatever reason, I was already towering over my parents by the time I reached junior high.

In fact, I was bigger than just about everyone on my basketball team, and I was also considerably better. My ability to "go to the hole" quickly went to my head. I was cocky, arrogant, and too big for my basketball britches. I vividly recall being in practice one day and thinking to myself, "This game is so easy for me that I don't even have to work hard at it." That was my attitude when I jogged through my wind sprints at the end of practice.

Fortunately, God has always put people in my life who refused to let me coast. Cliff Davis was one of those people. Davis was the first coach in my life who made me do what I didn't want to do so that I could be the person I wanted to be. Davis was such an influential part of my life that when I was inducted into the Texas A&M Athletics Hall of Fame in 2004, he was the one I chose to accept the award, since I couldn't be there because I was playing a game for the Cowboys that same weekend.

Davis, who had played college baseball at Texas A&M as a youngster, was a seasoned coach with a great smile and a better sense of humor. He also demanded the best of his players, and he had an amazing way of getting his message across immediately. He saw me loafing, and he knew my basketball success was going to my head. I'm so thankful that he took that moment to put me in my place. We were running sprints called "horses." I personally believe it would be better to label them as "dogs," because you will be dog tired after a few of them. You start at the baseline, run to the free-throw line, and then run back to the baseline. You then immediately turn around and run to half-court and back. Then you run to the other free-throw line and back, and finally you run to the other baseline and back. That's one horse. At a full sprint, one horse will send your heart pumping and your lungs expanding. But I was testing my boundaries, and I believed I was bigger than the team. Instead of sprinting, I was jogging. Coach Davis immediately called me aside and said, "Dat, you are going to run these horses at the same speed as everyone else. Get back out there and run them hard."

I nodded, but I actually thought, "What is he going to do to me? I'm the best player on this team." So, I went right back out and ran the next horse again at half speed and kind of looked at Coach Davis as I finished. I guess I expected a tirade or an exasperated look. I never expected the actual words that came out of his mouth. He said, "Dat, go to the locker room, get your uniform, and leave it on my desk. Get out of this gym. Now!" I was stunned, and my teammates were shocked. But I still had too much pride and far too much stubbornness to admit I was wrong. I sulked off the court, mumbled a few choice words, and put my uniform on his desk. I figured he would come crawling back to me the next day, begging me, the star of the roster, to return to the team. I figured wrong. I waited two days for Coach Davis to come crawling back to me. On the third day, I checked my pride at his office door and tucked my tail between my legs as I asked him for another chance. He agreed to let me back on the team, but there were several conditions. First, I had to sprint all the horses I had jogged on the day I was kicked off the team. Then, I had to apologize to each of my teammates individually. Finally, I had to run the normal horses with the rest of the team at the end of that day's practice. By the end of the day, I felt as though I was not only running horses but also carrying a Clydesdale on my back. I was beat, but I was back on the team, and I had learned a valuable lesson I have never forgotten.

I wish every kid could have a Coach Davis in his life. We all need to be encouraged, and that's precisely what Coach Davis did on most days. Of course, most of us also need to be put in our place from time to time, and that's exactly what he did on that particular day. I can't honestly say I have never gone half speed during a wind sprint since then, but I can say I have never again selfishly and arrogantly put myself before the team. Being kicked off my junior high basketball team for three days may seem like a fairly insignificant event to some. To me, it was a defining moment. It made me look at myself in the mirror and realize I had no one to blame but myself. I couldn't claim that I didn't care, either. I tried to tell myself that I didn't need him or the team. But truthfully, I loved being part of that team, and I admired Coach Davis much more than I was initially willing to admit. That little encounter taught me a valuable lesson I have never forgotten: If you want to taste glory, you first have to swallow pride. I did, and I became a better player, a better teammate, and a much better leader because of it. I also realized that Coach Davis had my best interest in mind, which is why I finally began to fall for football.

Coach Davis and Jimmy Hattenbach Sr. are good friends, and both of them had been encouraging me to give football a try throughout seventh grade. Basically, every time I saw Coach Davis in the hallways at school, he would push and prod me into giving the gridiron a go. Jimmy Sr. was doing the same thing when I would go over to Little Jimmy's house to eat or hang out, which was pretty much every day. I don't know why I was initially so reluctant. Maybe it was that pride thing again. Subconsciously, I didn't want people telling me what I should or shouldn't do. Perhaps it was also some of my own anxieties. As I said before, there was a sentiment among many people in Rockport and Fulton that the "gooks" may be good in soccer, but they'll never make it in a real sport like football. I may have had some lingering doubts of my own. What if I wasn't any good on the football field? What if "they" were right about the Vietnamese not being able to cut it on the football field? Was I really willing to prove them wrong or right?

At the urging of Coach Davis and Jimmy Hattenbach Sr., I finally decided as an eighth-grader to give it a shot. I knew I was big enough, unlike many of my Vietnamese friends and relatives. And from my experiences on the soccer field, I knew I was athletic enough. My concerns about being good enough were alleviated after the first few days of practice. I was already weighing about 180 pounds as an eighth-grader, which made me roughly 30 to 40 pounds heavier than most of the other kids I played with and against. For my weight, I owe a great deal of gratitude to Glenda Hattenbach and her famous King Ranch casserole. While my kin were eating rice with chopsticks, I was eating King Ranch casserole by the pound. Glenda was a great cook, and I remember stuffing myself on her fried chicken, pizza, pasta, Mexican food, and the casserole that still gets my taste buds watering. The Hattenbachs weren't wealthy anyway, but they nearly went broke feeding Little Jimmy and me. We would go through at least one gallon of milk per day and about five gallons of ice cream per week. Fortunately, my metabolism was as quick as a waterbug. I ate like a pig but remained as lean as a racehorse. When I stepped onto the football field for the first time ever, I was rather intimidating and completely at ease. Even when I made mistakes, I was strong enough, big enough, and quick enough to make a mess out of the opponents' game plan. And, unlike what I did in the basketball season that followed, I never went half speed.

I felt as though I had something to prove on the football field, and I showed up every day with the same passion for practice that some players reserved only for game day. In fact, perhaps I practiced with more passion than even Coach Davis, who was also our football coach, expected. I recall one practice about midway through my eighth-grade season when we were in position to win the school's first district championship in decades. People in town were already talking about how they couldn't wait to see my group when we were juniors and seniors in high school. It also appeared that we were going to be even better when a big kid moved to town from Arkansas. He was well over 200 pounds, and Coach Davis later told me that he thought this kid was manna from heaven, arriving at the midway point to bolster our offensive line. The kid said he had been a starting tackle in Arkansas, and everybody, including me, was excited about his joining the roster. At the start of his first practice, Coach Davis decided to see how tough the guy was, so he gave him the ball in a little drill where all the action takes place between parallel tackling dummies. It was basically a drill designed to get the linebackers accustomed to having running backs cutting back into the hole. Well, I jumped in there opposite the big kid because I too wanted to see how tough he was. I also wanted to see if I was tough enough to bring him down. Coach Davis gave him the ball and blew his whistle. All of a sudden, the big guy started screaming like a wild man, snarling his face and running toward me. I don't remember where exactly I made contact with him, but the collision was violent, and I remember hearing a loud snap. I tried to help him up, but his leg was broken in two. I truly felt bad that I had hurt the guy, especially since it came on his first play of his first practice.

But I also realized that injuries are a part of the game, and I concluded that the best way to avoid them was to be going at full speed all the time. In fact, my biggest problem in that first football season was learning how to play under control and not to overrun the ball carrier. Once I got that down, I was tough to contain. I was bigger and stronger than most of the linemen, and my legend had begun to grow. People in town spread the news of how I had broken some big kid's leg on his first day of practice, and more and more people came out to watch us play. I was blessed with good instincts on the field, and I became a student of the game. Most of all, I loved the contact. I didn't just try to hit a ball carrier; I tried to explode into him with every ounce of energy and muscle I had in my body. Since I was already much heavier than most of the running backs I played against, the results often produced oohs and ahhhs from the fans and my teammates. I remember on the first play of one game where I burst through the line of scrimmage and hit the tailback just as he was taking the ball from the quarterback. He went flying backward about five yards and landed flat on his butt. Seconds later, I looked toward their huddle and saw him shaking his head back and forth. I couldn't hear what he said, but I could read his lips as he told the quarterback, "I don't want the damn ball. You take it." Once I had the intimidation factor on my side, it was really pretty easy to make an impact on an opponent's game plan. I've always tried to read the opposition's eyes on the field, and I remember seeing some antsy expressions on the faces of quarterbacks and running backs. The bottom line is that I played with passion and was really having fun on the field.

By the time I reached Rockport-Fulton High School, I already had a reputation as a ferocious hitter and a freak of nature. My brother Hung, who is two years older than I am, was every bit as tough and instinctive as I was on the field. But as a senior, Hung played center at 5-foot-4, 140 pounds. Thanks to God's grace and Glenda Hattenbach's cooking, I played my senior season at Rockport at 5-foot-11, 230 pounds. I continued to be a student of the game, watching films and working on my techniques. And we continued to get better as a team. We were a Class 3A high school, and we began filling up that little, five thousand–seat stadium on Friday nights in the fall. I was selected as the 1993 District 30-3A Defensive Player of the Year as a senior and was also chosen as the All-South Texas Defensive Player of the Year by the *Corpus Christi Caller Times*. I even made second-team All-State as a punter. We made regional headlines and were the darlings of the community, as we fought and scratched our way into the Class 3A playoffs. Local businesses painted their storefronts with our green and gold school colors. The marquees in town read things like, "Go Pirates," and "Rockport-Fulton is Rock-Solid." It was crazy, and it was a lot of fun. I remember looking up into the stands on the November Friday night when we clinched the playoff berth and seeing all the joyous faces of the fans and residents of our community. There wasn't a Vietnamese section and a white section and a black section. They were all together, and—at least on Friday nights—we were no longer a community divided. I'm sure time had something to do with the healing and unifying that took place in Rockport-Fulton. But our football team expedited the process.

People from all races and backgrounds came to cheer for us. White men exchanged high-fives with Vietnamese boys when I made a big tackle. African American women embraced Vietnamese women when we made a big play. To be a fan of the 1993 Pirates meant that you were often cheering for that Vietnamese kid at middle linebacker. At least subconsciously, it also meant you had to accept me as a contributing part of the community. Many of those folks who cheered for me in high school were probably some of the same people who had refused to applaud for my youth soccer team six years earlier. That was fine with me. In fact, it probably made it more meaningful. But most meaningful was the fact that it wasn't just about me. Maybe I was a catalyst because of the headlines I earned or the plays I made. But my success on the football field brought cultures together one night a week during the fall and encouraged people to look each other in the eye the rest of the days of the week. It also encouraged many of the Vietnamese kids to branch out and to make themselves part of the community and part of the magical world of athletics. When I began playing high school football at Rockport-Fulton, about 5 percent of the Vietnamese kids in the school were participating in high school athletics. By the time I graduated, nearly 30 percent of the Asian kids at Rockport-Fulton were playing sports. I'm more proud of that than of any award I ever received in high school. Today, there are probably more than two thousand people of Vietnamese descent living in the Rockport-Fulton area. Generally speaking, they are viewed as good neighbors and contributing members of the local economy. And there's not much doubt that the former refugees have added to the community's overall culture.

I helped to make a difference in Rockport-Fulton. For the most part, I did it by making a friend and becoming part of something bigger than myself. One person can make a difference, but a team is capable of making miracles happen. That's the true beauty of sports. The billboard on the outskirts of town is of me, but I Remember the Pirates. I love what we accomplished on the field and the lasting effect it had on the community. The games we won will eventually be forgotten, but the people we won over will never forget.

CHAPTER 6

Texas A&M's Big, Fat Failure

ONE OF THE MORE MEANINGFUL compliments I've ever received came from a man I barely even knew. Retired Maj. Gen. Ted Hopgood, a two-star general in the Marine Corps, was the commandant of the Corps of Cadets at Texas A&M when I was in college. Our paths rarely crossed on the sprawling College Station campus, but we did share something of a bond in terms of our understanding of the Vietnamese culture. A 1965 graduate of Texas A&M, Hopgood served three tours as an infantry officer in Vietnam from 1965 to 1971. His time in Vietnam brought him face-to-face with the Vietcong, the North Vietnamese Army, the South Vietnamese war personnel, and the people of South Vietnam. Hopgood is a real hero and a highly respected leader of men in every sense, so I was blown away when I first read some of the glowing things he had to say about me in an interview with *12th Man Magazine*.

"If I had been able to play college football, I like to believe I would have attempted to play like Dat," said Hopgood, also a huge fan of A&M football and all Aggie sports. "I admired his heart and determination. He personified what the Aggie spirit and Aggie football is all about. The fact he is Vietnamese also is of significance to me because the determination and the fighting spirit I saw Dat display in every game is what I remember about the very strong feelings I had about the Vietnamese people. The North Vietnamese and the Vietcong soldiers my troops went up against were fantastically dedicated and skilled soldiers. I can say the same thing about many of the South Vietnamese soldiers and Marines I served with. Dat epitomizes the determination and never-give-up spirit I encountered in fighting with and against the Vietnamese people."

Pretty impressive, huh? But now that I have patted myself on the back, I feel compelled to let you in on the truth: It's a good thing General Hopgood never saw me practicing during my early days at A&M. It's an even better thing that he couldn't have read my mind back then. Had he known me or seen me then, he would have likely taken one look at me and drawn some dramatically different conclusions—probably the same conclusions many of the Texas A&M coaches were reaching about me. Among the most prominent questions the coaches were asking themselves about me was, "Why in the world did we ever sign this guy?"

When I first arrived at Texas A&M in the summer of 1994, my fighting spirit and never-give-up attitude were more comparable to the Pillsbury Doughboy than the Vietnamese soldiers Hopgood remembered. My midsection was about as round as the Michelin Man, while my upper body drooped like the branches of a weeping willow tree. After signing a national letter-of-intent to attend Texas A&M in February of 1994, I celebrated by eating. In the next few months, I rarely stopped eating. My primary method of training for my career as a college football player was pumping silverware, not iron. My main cardiovascular activity during this time consisted of laps to the refrigerator, and my only speed work revolved around "fast" food. I ate with a passion and a purpose, and I really didn't have any regrets.

Besides simply not knowing how to take care of my body, I had convinced myself I was doing what I was supposed to do in order to become a big-time college football player. The recruiting services and so-called experts had said and written that I probably needed to be bigger in order to play inside linebacker at Texas A&M. I listened and used that as an excuse to stuff my face as much as I possibly could. Instead of getting bigger by adding muscle, however, I just got fatter, lazier, slower, and softer. By the time I showed up at Texas A&M and began practicing in the summer of '94, I was tipping the scales at almost 240 pounds of mostly fat. My uniform was tight, my quickness was disappearing, and my ability to make the plays I was so accustomed to making in high school was gone. I looked bad in the mirror, but I looked even worse on film. I moved with all the precision, speed, and grace of a beached whale. As I looked around the practice field and evaluated the talent on the team, I quickly concluded that I might be the worst defensive player on the roster. Even many of the walk-ons were better than I was. It was quite clear from the start that I would red-shirt in 1994 and not play any of my first year. But I also wondered if I would ever play at Texas A&M. Most of all, I wondered if I had made a major mistake by coming to A&M in the first place.

The more I dwelt on my dilemma, the more I ate. The more I ate, the worse I felt. The worse I felt, the less I cared about football and the more I wanted out of Texas A&M. I was fat, but I definitely wasn't happy. In fact, I was a miserable, unmotivated mess, and I came fairly close to making a major mistake that would undoubtedly have altered my life in a significant and negative way. I was feeling so sorry for myself—and trying so hard to keep from blaming myself for my situation—that I decided I was going to teach Texas A&M a lesson by either transferring to Michigan or quitting altogether. "Yeah," I thought to myself, "they'll be sorry for not giving me more of a chance. They are really screwing this thing up."

In reality, of course, I was the one who was "screwing this thing up," but it took me a while to come to that conclusion. For so much of my adolescence, I had battled to be accepted. I wanted desperately to prove to people that I did belong on a football field. I wanted to prove all the doubters, the name-callers, the pessimists, and the racists wrong. In many ways, they were my primary motivation, and every insult or skeptical comment added fuel to my fire. Then when I was being recruited and continually patted on the back by college coaches and scouts, I initially found it difficult to handle being so widely accepted. I know that sounds a bit bizarre, but it's a problem many athletes face. It's actually pretty easy to train, to focus, and even to push yourself beyond your normal breaking point when someone is doubting or "dissing" you. But when everybody seems to be constantly singing your praises, it's so much easier to lose your focus. It's hard to maintain your drive if you begin feeling like you've arrived. In my opinion, that's why it is so difficult for teams—at any level—to repeat as champions.

In any event, when the major college football programs across the country began calling me every night and coming to my house in hopes of landing my services, I lost my sense of purpose. Or, at the very least, I lost my edge. I was enjoying the moment, and I let the attention go to my head and everything else go to my waistline. I was tasting the good life and asking for second and third helpings. I never lost sight of the fact that I was the son of a shrimper, but I was suddenly thrust into the world of lobster feasts. I had never eaten lobster before, but that's exactly what I was treated to on recruiting trips to Michigan and UCLA. Whether I admitted it to myself or not, I figured I had officially arrived.

From my personal experience, I can say that a man who is not constantly stretching and expanding his dreams is a man who will soon lose sight of them. During much of 1994, I definitely lost sight of my dreams. I guess I eventually stretched out my pants enough that I finally forced myself to re-evaluate my dreams and redefine my goals. But it took some tough lessons and some long, lonely nights for me to finally realize that attaining your heart's desire can sometimes be just as dangerous as losing it. I remember reading a devotional once that stated, "Lord, grant that I may always desire more than I accomplish." I didn't really know what that meant at the time, but I have a much better understanding now. It takes humility to realize that accomplished dreams—no matter how big or small—are merely stepping stones; they are not a final destination.

I didn't have much humility following my senior season in high school. I may not have been outwardly boastful, but I was inwardly filled with pride in what I had accomplished. The recruiting process only added to my pride. Recruiting is purely about vanity, not humility. Over and over again, I was told how great I was, how perfect I was for this school or that one, and how important I was to the future plans of this university or that one. My pride swelled each time I heard it, and I quickly began to believe it. It wouldn't take long for me to receive a first-hand lesson on pride going before a fall. I would eventually fall pretty hard, but let me describe the recruiting-induced rise to prominence I went through in my own mind.

My first opportunity to make a big impression on the college football recruiters came during one of my high school basketball games. In those tight tank tops and short shorts, I looked like a lighter-skinned version of Charles Barkley—the original round mound of rebound. Despite my pudginess, I was actually a pretty good high school basketball player, and I later received one scholarship offer to play college basketball from the University of Texas at San Antonio. I averaged nineteen points a game as a center during my senior season at Rockport, and I could dunk the basketball with at least some degree of authority. I wasn't Michael Jordan, but I did have some "hops." But during November of 1993 my focus was primarily on making an impression on the big boys of college football. Prior to one of our home basketball games, I learned I had my chance that night. Football coaches from Michigan and Notre Dame were going to be in the crowd to watch me play that evening. Because of NCAA rules, they couldn't talk to me on that particular night. But they were there to evaluate my athleticism, and I was a little more nervous than usual. Early in the game, I was fouled and went to the free-throw line. Instead of focusing on the free throws, I was wondering how to impress these coaches. My next move was quite unimpressive, as I uncorked an airball from the free-throw line. That should have been my first lesson in humility, but I didn't pause long enough to ponder such things back then.

Besides, those coaches must have seen at least some glimmer of hope in me. Former Michigan head coach Gary Moehler was the first coach to come calling on me, showing up at my house in Rockport on December 1, 1993—the first day college coaches could contact prospects—to offer me the chance of a lifetime. I honestly didn't grow up as a big college football fan, but I did occasionally envision myself in the maize and blue of Michigan when I played backyard ball with family members. Even as a relatively unknowledgeable college football fan, I certainly knew about the "Big House," Michigan's 100,000-seat home stadium. I also knew about the school's great fight song and the one-of-a-kind helmets the Wolverines wore with such intimidation. As ridiculous as this may sound, I was initially leaning toward Michigan in large part because of how cool I thought the helmets looked. Of course, I also knew about some of the star players who had made a lasting impression in those helmets—guys like Heisman Trophy winner Desmond Howard, three-time All-American Anthony Carter, and a young linebacker by the name of Jarrett Irons.

Any reluctance I had about going so far away from home was eased by Moehler's description of Irons. A year earlier, Moehler had convinced Irons to leave his home in The Woodlands, Texas, (just north of Houston) for Ann Arbor. Irons was an immediate success, breaking into the starting lineup as a freshman in 1993. Moehler told me I had a chance to be the next Jarrett Irons, and I was impressed enough to agree to make Michigan one of my official recruiting trips. Besides, I wondered somehow if Michigan might have been some kind of destiny for me. After all, my family's first real home in the United States was in Michigan following my birth in the refugee camp in Arkansas. I believe in signs, and I thought Moehler's emergence on my doorstep might have been some kind of sign from above that I should at least look into making Michigan my home once again. The offer to visit Michigan also meant I would be making my first-ever plane trip.

My knees were practically buckling when I boarded the plane in Corpus Christi for my first flight. Once we got off the ground, though, my nerves calmed as I began envisioning myself in the maize and blue. I figured I would be impressed with Michigan, but when I stepped foot off the plane in Detroit, I was blown away. Everything about my visit was first-class. The coaches were great, the players were down to earth, and the coeds were beautiful. So was the snow. I had never remembered seeing snow before, and I was treated to a blanket of white powder covering the Michigan campus. I also had a meal fit for a king, which included fresh Maine lobster and corn-fed beef. As an added bonus, I also had a chance to catch a Michigan home basketball game featuring most of the famous Fab Five. Chris Weber was already gone, so it was the Fab Four at that time. Still, it was fabulous. In fact, my entire trip to Michigan was so exceptional that I gave a verbal commitment to Moehler before I went back home.

In recruiting, verbal commitments are non-binding, which means they are often about as worthless as a losing lottery ticket. In the realm of college recruiting, kids change their minds nearly as often as they change their underwear. But at least in my mind, I was fairly certain that Michigan was for me. I even bought a Michigan sweatshirt on my way out of town. I gave my commitment to the Wolverines and went home. But I wasn't about to give up my other trips. As I mentioned earlier, the trip to Ann Arbor had provided me with my first opportunity to fly. One week later, I had another trip scheduled that involved another flight. Instead of going north again, I went west to Los Angeles. To be perfectly honest, I didn't have much serious interest in UCLA, especially after the incredible trip I had made to Michigan. But I felt I owed it to myself to at least explore other possibilities, and I definitely wanted to be treated like a king again.

Upon my arrival in Los Angeles, I was once again given the royal treatment. I thought the bundled-up Michigan coeds were cute, but when I got to the UCLA campus I suddenly understood the Beach Boys' inspiration for the lyrics "I wish they all could be California girls." In addition to the glitz and glamour of L.A., I was amazed at the scenery of it all. During my weekend trip, we stayed in a hotel where you could see water from one side of the hotel and the mountains from another vantage point. My hosts (on each recruiting trip you are hosted by a current player or two) also drove me around Los Angeles, and I was star-struck by Rodeo Drive, the palm trees and everything else I had previously seen only on TV. I once again ate lobster, and I suddenly began picturing myself in the powder blue and gold of UCLA. Incidentally, powder blue may be the ugliest uniform color in all of college football, but I was loving the star treatment I received in the shadows of Hollywood.

I didn't change my commitment from Michigan to UCLA, but when I was leaving Los Angeles, I was no longer completely convinced that Ann Arbor was the only possible place for me. I decided I needed to keep my options open and to base my decision on more meaningful matters than helmet designs and lobster buffets. I also decided that if I ever wanted my family and friends in Rockport to watch me play in person, I probably needed to look at schools much closer to home. So, I cancelled trips I had planned to Notre Dame and Florida and decided I would take two other trips, to Texas and Texas A&M.

If you are not from the Lone Star State, you may be under the impression that Texas and Texas A&M are similar schools. Even some folks in Texas may have that misconception. But aside from the facts that both schools have big enrollments and both take a great deal of pride in their football programs, they are extremely different universities. Texas A&M sits at the heart of a college community; Texas is located in the middle of a large city. Texas students tend to be more liberal than the conservative students of Aggieland. Texas A&M has grown from a small, all-male military school in the 1960s to a huge, world-class university; Texas has long been a giant university with a powerhouse football program. Texas students boast about all the live bands on Sixth Street; Texas A&M students boast about the best marching band in the nation.

I could go on and on. And the arguments between the rabid fans can become extremely heated depending on how many beers have been consumed and how close it is to Thanksgiving, when the Aggies and Longhorns meet for state bragging rights. In reality, both schools are outstanding in their own right. But when I visited the two schools, I immediately realized A&M was right for me; Texas was not. Coming from a small town, I felt right at home at Texas A&M. While Bryan–College Station doesn't have many bright lights, it does feature plenty of attractions. In fact, it's much bigger than Rockport-Fulton with much more to do. But it also has an intimate feeling to it, which I quickly and thoroughly enjoyed. The A&M campus was also the friendliest piece of real estate I had ever encountered. To walk across the A&M campus is like taking a trip into a western movie set. I had never heard the word "Howdy" spoken so many times in all my life, and it made me feel right at home.

As much as I loved Texas A&M, I do have to give Texas and former head coach John Mackovic credit for their efforts. The Longhorns tried to make me feel at home by introducing me to a very well-endowed Asian girl, who served as my tour guide of the campus and my hostess for the weekend. It was quite obvious she had been hand-picked by the Texas coaches to make me feel at ease, and it was obvious to me that the Longhorns were operating under the old advertising theme, "Sex sells." She never made any advances toward me, but her large chest and tight sweaters were eye-catching, to say the least. So were the "interesting" folks I encountered on the streets of Austin.

In the end, my selection of A&M over Texas, however, had nothing to do with Austin's nightlife versus College Station's conservatism. I simply felt that Texas A&M was more suited for me as a football player. Mackovic was known as an offensive innovator, and on my trip to Texas, it was obvious to me his focus was primarily on offense. In particular, his focus was on Jerod Douglas, the record-setting tailback from Converse Judson High School, just outside San Antonio. Douglas rushed for 6,189 yards during his high school career, and he helped to lead Judson to Class 5A state championships in 1992 and 1993. He was a little guy (5-foot-9), but he had made a big name in high school. Douglas made his recruiting trip to Texas the same weekend I was in Austin, and the Longhorns put on a dog and pony show to try to impress him.

I guess it didn't work. Douglas ended up signing with Baylor and enjoyed a good career in Waco, becoming the school's second all-time leading rusher. But what I gathered from Texas' treatment of Douglas was that the Longhorns were primarily intent on building an offensive juggernaut. If they happened to sign a few good defensive players along the way, that would be icing on the cake. Although Mackovic seemed like a nice guy, we never really made a connection.

I found it much easier to make a connection with the coaching staff at Texas A&M, partly because of the school's priority on great defensive football and partly because of the genuine nature of the staff, although I did realize I was not the Aggies' top priority in the 1994 recruiting class. Head coach R. C. Slocum was supposed to come to my house in Rockport one night for a visit, but he called me and told me something had come up at A&M so he would not be able to be out of town that evening. Well, what had actually come up was an awards dinner in Houston to honor A&M lineman Sam Adams. While in Houston, Slocum also visited Trent Driver, another linebacker A&M was recruiting. I found out about it when the evening news featured the awards dinner with Slocum smiling in the background. Of course, even I couldn't blame Slocum for spending some time with Adams and Driver instead of me. Driver was a high school All-American and one of the most coveted linebacker prospects in the country. Most recruiting experts rated him as the headliner of Texas A&M's 1994 recruiting class. Driver was a man among boys in high school, and I certainly didn't hold a grudge against Slocum. Shoot, I kind of thought that it was at least nice of Slocum to be vague instead of telling me the truth, which would have been something like, "Hey Dat, I can't make it down to Rockport tonight. Trent Driver is a heck of a lot better prospect than you, so I need to secure him a little more before I even worry about you."

In my one-on-one meetings and telephone discussions with Slocum, he came across as a folksy guy. He came from rather humble beginnings, and he possessed a down-home demeanor. In my opinion, Slocum was never really a master motivator, but he was excellent in recruiting because he could speak in a tone and language that made the player and his parents feel comfortable. Of course, my parents presented a much different challenge because they barely spoke English. My parents actually thought the whole recruiting process was a practical joke. They could not fathom why any university would care so much about football— or any other sport, for that matter—to pay for student-athletes to receive an education, room and board, meals, etc. Coming from Vietnam, where higher education was a pipe dream for most of the population, my mother and father kept waiting for the catch—as in, "What's the catch?" I would tell them that I had an opportunity to go to Michigan, UCLA, Texas A&M, Texas, or various other schools, and in the Vietnamese equivalent, their response would usually be something like: "Get real, Dat."

Speaking of real, that's the feeling I got from the people of Texas A&M. There wasn't any snow on the ground and there were no mountain ranges on the horizon in College Station. There wasn't a nearby beach or a thriving downtown area, either. And compared to going to the basketball game at Michigan, A&M's old arena—G. Rollie White Coliseum (which has been replaced now)—looked merely mundane. But I simply felt more comfortable at A&M. My host for the weekend trip to Texas A&M was Brad Crowley, who was from Corpus Christi. Being raised along the Texas coast, I had heard of Crowley, and I knew he was a solid linebacker. (Crowley later moved to the defensive line and was a key factor in helping us win the Big 12 South title in 1997). Crowley and his roommate, kicker Kyle Bryant, showed me around the campus and were prepared to take me out on the town. But I remember being so sold on the people of Texas A&M and the reputation of the Aggies' defense that I didn't need to explore the nightlife to make my decision. I had been wined and dined at other schools, but at A&M, I just kind of wanted to be alone with my thoughts. Crowley asked me what I wanted to do, and I told him I simply wanted to grab a cheeseburger and go back to the hotel.

After I threw down my cheeseburger, I went back to my room and began flipping through the pages of the Texas A&M media guide. A&M may not have been as high profile as some of the other schools I was considering, but I liked the way it felt, and it had something I definitely wanted to be a part of—the "Wrecking Crew" defense. An A&M defensive back, Chet Brooks, coined the Wrecking Crew moniker in the mid-1980s, and it had gained national publicity thanks in large part to the aggressive, ball-hawking play of the Aggie linebackers. Former A&M linebackers like John Roper, Aaron Wallace, Quentin Coryatt, William Thomas, and Marcus Buckley had been so dominant in College Station that A&M had earned the reputation of the "Linebacker U of the South." Penn State may have been the original Linebacker U, but Texas A&M was producing some prolific playmakers at the position. I prayed about it; I talked to my parents and friends about it; and I eventually determined that A&M was the right place for me. The defensive reputation, the genuineness of the coaching staff and the A&M people, and the proximity to my hometown all led me to decide that wearing the maroon and white was right for me.

I was not, however, the only linebacker in the Lone Star State who came to that conclusion. On the first Wednesday of February in 1994, I signed my national letter of intent to play at Texas A&M. So did four other fantastic linebackers in Texas. Headlined by Trent Driver and Warrick Holdman, the '94 line-backing class was labeled as the "Fab Five" by several recruiting services and sportswriters, and the overall recruiting class was ranked in the top 10 nationally by several recruiting services. I was part of that class, but I wasn't really in the same class as the others. Of the five linebackers—Driver, Holdman, Quinton Brown, Phillip Meyers, and me—I was probably the least known and the least important. The only reason I received any attention at all was because of my Vietnamese descent and my last name. In Vietnam, the name "Nguyen" is about as common as Johnson is in the United States. But in college football circles, it was about as unusual and distinctive as Michael Jackson's surgically altered nose. The pronunciations of my name ranged from "Nu-jin" to "Nu-gee-an." But after I signed with A&M, at least some people were trying to pronounce my name. In fact, even *Sports Illustrated* was writing it.

In the magazine's summer college football preview, I was the subject of a one-page feature story on freshmen impact players. There was a picture of me in shorts and a Texas A&M T-shirt, sitting on the shrimp-boat dock and holding two crabs. The cut-line of the picture read, "The Texas A&M linebacker will be sinking his claws into Aggie opponents." In the story, my high school head coach, Bob Pyssen, compared me to former Baylor All-American and Chicago Bears All-Pro middle linebacker Mike Singletary. It was a short, but very complimentary article that was written more because of my Vietnamese descent than because of what I was expected to do in the fall. Because of my immaturity, I let the article and sudden fame go to my head. Publicly, I said it was no big deal. In my mind, though, I thought, "*Sports Illustrated!* Hot damn. I really am the man. I've already made a name for myself."

When I showed up at A&M in the summer weighing about 240 pounds, however, the Aggie coaches found few reasons to even bother calling my name. When I arrived at A&M, I was so fat and out of shape that some of the players assumed I had been recruited as a punter. We actually had one punter who was a little heavy, but I was downright fat. And I could have summed up my chances of making an immediate impact at A&M in two words: fat chance. Four of the linebackers—Driver, Brown, Holdman, and Meyers—from the so-called "Fab Five" recruiting class played as true freshmen, although Holdman later suffered an injury and was redshirted. At least Holdman had already turned the heads of A&M coaches. I, on the other hand, mainly just turned the stomachs of our coaches. Early in my freshman season, several A&M fans asked recruiting coordinator Tim Cassidy how the freshman class was shaping up. He told them that all of the guys were looking good, and they probably had made only one mistake in the class. I'll give you one guess as to who the mistake was. I can't blame Cassidy or any of the other coaches who had that opinion of me. After all, I was of the same opinion. And I was concluding that coming to A&M was a big mistake.

The 1994 season was a good one for the Aggies. We were on a one-year probation that prevented us from being on TV, participating in a bowl game, or competing for the Southwest Conference championship. Despite the probation cloud hanging over us, we rolled to a 10-0-1 record with the only blemish coming in an embarrassing tie against SMU. But while it was a good season for the team, it began as a miserable one for me. On the practice field, I initially moved about as slowly as a slug in salt. The only thing I mastered early on was the buffet line at Cain Dining Hall. At one point in the season, I think I was the number-eight linebacker on the depth chart. The only reason I wasn't any lower was because there weren't nine linebackers at my inside position. I was seriously considering a transfer or simply going back home and calling it quits. I didn't talk it over much with anybody, primarily because I was too embarrassed to admit how bad I was to any friends from home or my parents.

The only real talking I did was with God. I wasn't very spiritually mature at the time, but I was asking—or begging—God to give me a sign to show me what I needed to do. I was actually hoping God would write me a message in the clouds that said, "Go to Michigan" or "Stay at A&M." In my personal experiences, though, God is rarely that straightforward. I asked for a sign showing me what I needed to do, and it was provided for me in the most unlikely of places—the sports section of the *Bryan/College Station Eagle*. During two-a-days in 1994, a picture of me appeared on the front page of the sports section. I looked at it, studied it, and eventually understood what I needed to do about it. I looked like one of the "before" pictures in a SlimFast or Subway sandwiches commercial. My arms were fat, my face was fat, and my gut was hanging out from my jersey and over the belt loop on my practice pants.

The picture made me sick at my stomach. It also became a lasting and motivating image to me. Ever since my final high school game, I had spent almost every waking moment feeling either too good about myself or sorry for myself. I had gotten lazy and fat. I guess I could have figured that out by looking in the mirror, but it had a much more dramatic effect on me in the newspaper—where everyone in the Bryan–College Station area received an eyeful of Fat Dat. With that image as my motivation, I knew exactly what I needed to do. I didn't have any illusions of becoming a superstar at A&M, but I made a vow to myself that I would no longer be Fat Dat. It was time to begin some serious reshaping—physically, mentally, spiritually, and beyond. It was time to discover that "fighting spirit" General Hopgood noticed in the jungles of Vietnam. It was time to quit moping and start moving.

CHAPTER 7

Labels Are for Canned Goods

As you might imagine, many people—especially witty newspaper headline and cutline writers—love to have fun with my name. I've seen and heard plenty of puns and pronunciation plays on words through the years. There's the "Win-Nguyen" situation, the "Nguyen-ing Edge," "Nguyen-Breaker" and the "Who? What? Where? And Nguyen." That's just my last name. There have been plenty of creative catch-phrases with my first name, as well. Such as: "Dat-A-Way," "Dat's More Like It," and "This and Dat." I even sometimes refer to myself as Aubrey's "Datty." But the most effective use of my name was, fittingly, created by the people who named me in the first place: my parents.

The hostilities toward the Vietnamese shrimpers along the Texas coast in the late 1970s and early 1980s eventually led my father out of the shrimping industry. When I was in the fourth grade (1983–84), he sold his boat and built the Hong Kong Restaurant. Various family members helped him build the restaurant, which had virtually everything except a good location. That, of course, was a recipe for disaster. The restaurant, which was located away from the main highway, would draw big crowds on Sundays because of the buffet. But during the week, business was extremely slow. It was so slow during the week that I was often the primary customer. My mother used to joke that I ate her out of business by eating all the leftovers on hand after the limited traffic into the restaurant six days a week. My mother and father poured everything—time, money, resources—into the Hong Kong Restaurant for two years, but ultimately, it was a financial drain on them. They sold the restaurant to another family member, and my dad went back to work on a shrimping boat for some time and later built a marine supply store in Fulton.

But my father always believed he could make a living in the restaurant business, and when I started making a name for myself on the football field in high school and college, he and my mother made another run at the food industry with Hu-Dat Restaurant. The name is actually a combination of my name and my brother Hung's name. I'm biased in my critique, of course, but it is an outstanding restaurant that has become a landmark of sorts and a tourist's destination in Rockport-Fulton. It was a success right from the start because the food was good and the location—near the waterfront in Fulton—was much better than the first attempt. With each story that came out about me, the restaurant also received free publicity.

Reporters are always looking for interesting angles for their stories, and my route to Texas A&M featured more angles than some geometry textbooks. Included in virtually every feature story that has ever been written about me was my family's escape from Vietnam, our cross-country journeys upon first arriving in the United States, my father's shrimping experiences, and my parents' restaurant just off the Fulton Beach fishing piers. My parents filled the front entry of the restaurant with some of my football memorabilia, including jerseys, trophies, newspaper clippings, and pictures, and business continued to pour in for lunch and dinner. Business was so good that my parents later opened other successful Hu-Dat locations in Corpus Christi and Ingleside, putting family members in charge of day-to-day operations.

In other words, most of my A&M teammates were quite familiar with Hu-Dat long before I ever began taking them to visit my hometown and experience the restaurant for themselves. Whenever I did take friends home, my parents would go all out to impress them with the quality and the quantity of food. Hu-Dat serves an affordable mix of Gulf seafood, popular Chinese food, and a small selection of authentic Vietnamese food. If you like noodles, rice, steamed vegetables, Chinese food, or fresh seafood, you'd probably love Hu-Dat. That's what I told my former teammates when we took a trip to Rockport together following my first season in the NFL in 2000.

I was trying to help my church in Rockport raise money by appearing at a Chinese New Year's banquet, and I thought it would also be a good time to share some of my culture and show off some of my childhood stomping grounds to friends Rich Coady, Koby Hackradt, and Toya Jones. Toya, a defensive back and an outstanding track athlete at A&M, grew up in nearby Refugio, Texas, so he knew plenty about Rockport-Fulton and the Vietnamese influence on the community. But Hackradt, an offensive lineman, was from Conroe, and Coady, a hard-hitting safety who won a Super Bowl ring with the St. Louis Rams during his rookie season in 1999, was from Dallas. So I knew this would be an entirely new and strange experience for them. I also knew that this was a perfect opportunity to have a little fun at their expense. I'm known for my pranks, and it was time to pull another one.

Rich and Koby were expecting the typical Hu-Dat cuisine, but at the church, which was our first stop for the Chinese New Year's celebration, they brought out authentic Vietnamese dishes that I knew would turn the stomachs of my former teammates, who were accustomed to less exotic selections. When we sat down for the meal, I purposely positioned Rich to my left and Koby on the other side of the table, so neither could hear what I was telling the other. I started with Rich, telling him that my family and friends had gone to a lot of trouble to prepare this authentic cuisine and that it would be disrespectful to all of us if he didn't eat it. I could barely keep from laughing as Rich nodded cautiously.

Then they brought a dish out in which very rare duck meat is put through a grinder. After the blood dries, it looks almost like pizza. One of the soups contained raw seafood that Rich later claimed was still moving. It's not all that different from authentic sushi, but for Rich, it was more than he could take. There were two hundred people in the church, and many of them were in on the joke, watching as Rich stared at his food for two minutes. Then I whispered to him, "Rich, if you really are my friend, you will eat this and not disrespect my family." He looked at it again, contemplated it, and actually touched it before he finally said, "Buddy, I don't want to disrespect anyone, and you are one of my best friends, but this stuff is just too nasty looking to put in my mouth."

I laughed and told him it was all part of a joke, but then I pulled the same story on Koby. Big-hearted, good-natured Koby fell for it hook, line, and sinker. I could tell he didn't want any part of it, but he picked up the nearly raw duck and tossed it in his mouth. When he swallowed it, he looked as though he had seen a ghost as he quickly tried to wash away the taste with a big glass of water. When he finally got it down and no longer looked as if he was going to puke, he said, "That was one of the nastiest, grossest things I've ever tasted. What was that crunchy stuff?" I looked at him seriously and told him it was cartilage. Koby nearly gagged again as the entire table burst into laughter.

The prank turned out as I had expected. It really wouldn't insult anyone if they chose not to eat any particular dish. But I figured if I poured it on thick enough for Koby, he would fall for the prank. I also figured Rich knew my sense of humor well enough to realize eventually that I was, indeed, pulling his leg. By that time, Rich and I knew each other about as well as anyone. We had spent countless hours during our five years at A&M together talking about everything from football aspirations to girlfriend frustrations. We would discuss deep topics of life, as well as two-deep coverages on the football field. I probably owe much of who I am today as a football player to the friendship Rich and I developed during the frustrations of our 1994 season.

As I mentioned previously, the 1994 season was a good one for the Aggies, as A&M went 10-0-1. For me personally, it began as a combination of homesickness, humble-pie, and hopelessness. But once I finally saw my "sign" in the newspaper and found my way out of a funk, I grew determined to shed the "Fat Dat" label. At about that same time, Rich and I became joined at the hip. He was a walk-on from Dallas Pearce High School, and I was a scholarship player at the cavernous end of the depth chart. I was the son of a shrimp-sized shrimper; his father, Richard, had played for the Chicago Bears from 1967 to 1975. He came from a neighborhood filled with SUVs; I came from a background where our neighbors were driven away by the NVA. While we had our differences, we had one thing in common: we both felt as though we had something to prove.

Rich has told me that his first impression of me was that I

must be lazy to be that fat. Once I made up my mind to reshape my body, however, the person I kept bumping into at Netum Steed—Texas A&M's weight room and conditioning lab—was Rich Coady. We would work out in the mornings; we'd work out in the afternoons; and if there was any other time left in the day, we'd usually spend it in the weight room. I could tell right away that Rich had an impressive work ethic that was going to carry him to greater heights. His philosophy regarding his workouts, then and now, was that he wasn't really satisfied with himself until he had pushed so hard that he was either throwing up or on the verge of it. Aside from the food I tried to get him to eat on our trip to Rockport, it took a lot to make Rich hurl. After a week or two of watching him and bumping into him, I decided that Rich and I needed to work out together. We both knew we weren't going to play in 1994, and we both realized we would need to do much more than the rest of our teammates to have a chance of ever stepping onto Kyle Field.

So we began bugging our strength and conditioning coach, Mike Clark, practically pleading with him to provide us with extra workouts that might give us some kind of additional edge. Coach Clark obliged, and Rich and I pushed each other beyond what either of us thought possible. We were always competing, seeing who could lift the most weight or do the most reps. Coach Clark devised a workout where we would put 220 pounds on the bar for a bench press, bring the weight down slowly, pause it on our chests for a second or two, and then slowly lift it off. You would continue to do reps until complete failure, which meant you could no longer remove the bar from your own chest and needed a spotter to help you place the bar back in the rack. Well, Rich was a particularly good bench presser, and he always went last. Inevitably, he would do one more rep than I did, which used to drive me crazy. But that type of competition also drove me to be better conditioned and better on the field.

After our marathon workouts, Rich and I would be soaked in sweat, exhausted, and often sick at our stomachs. We'd have to sit and talk for awhile just to allow our legs to regain their function and to let the queasy sensations in our stomachs pass. During those resting times, we would start talking about our goals for the future. As I recall, Rich's primary goal was to get on the field in a game situation someday. He wasn't initially focused on earning a scholarship as much as he was intent on playing in a game. Rich figured that all this work would be worth it if he managed to become a special teams player by his senior year. "I'd be happy just to cover kicks or block somebody on a punt return," Rich used to say. For me, the goal was to earn a starting inside linebacker spot by my senior season. The only reason I shot for my senior season was that I knew that Trent Driver would be gone by then. Driver could have been a cover boy for *Muscle & Fitness* magazine, and he played inside linebacker as a true freshman in '94. Looking at him, I believed Driver was born to play linebacker, and I figured I would always be in his shadow as long as he was at A&M.

So Rich and I busted our tails in the weight room, working out for hours a day five or six times a week in hopes that maybe by our senior season we would have some kind of significant role for the maroon and white in the game-day plans. But for the 1994 season, we were relegated to wearing the blue and white of the scout team. Being a redshirt or walk-on and playing on the scout team can be pretty tough because you are beaten up in practice all week, running the opponent's schemes against the first-string and second-team guys who will actually be playing on Saturday. In other words, it's all pain, no game.

Being on the scout team also creates a bit of a dilemma. If you bust your butt on every play and make the starters look bad, you run the risk of being ostracized by your teammates. But if you don't go hard on every play, you run the risk of not being noticed by the coaches or, worse, being labeled by the coaching staff as a loafer. I certainly didn't need to be labeled as a loafer since I already had a rather low reputation among some of the coaches because of how overweight and out of shape I was when I first reported to two-a-days. Our defensive coordinator and inside linebackers coach in 1994, Tommy Tuberville, seemed to have a particularly strong disdain for me because of my inability to make plays when I first reported. I was later told that Tuberville, in a staff meeting, informed the rest of the coaches that I would never play at Texas A&M. I sensed his seething eyes, heard his disapproving tone of voice, and figured I would one day find a collar hanging in my locker since I was so securely stationed in his doghouse.

But as Rich and I worked relentlessly on our conditioning and strength away from the field—and I started eating more fruits than fruitcakes—an amazing thing began happening to my performance on the field. I was moving better and more quickly than ever before, as my weight plummeted from 240 pounds to about 215 by late in the 1994 season. I avoided fried foods and treated the ice cream machine in Cain Hall like a pothole in the road, steering clear of virtually everything that would contribute to a "spare tire" around my midsection. Suddenly, the love handles were disappearing, and the "Fat Dat" label was no longer appropriate. Having shed the pounds, I was suddenly able to shed blockers with my quickness and agility. I certainly wasn't the fastest guy on the field, but I did have good quickness once I dropped the weight.

It's a good thing that Rich and I had developed such a good friendship because I didn't win many friends on the team for the rest of the year. I decided that I was going to play each day in practice the only way I really knew how to play: full speed. I had already made a positive impression on Coach Clark with my workout routine in the weight room, but probably the first positive impression I made on the rest of the coaching staff was as a member of the "Smurfs." (We were called that since we wore blue jerseys on the scout team.) Some of the offensive coaches began to take notice of me because of the way I was making plays against our first-team offense. Mike Clark later told me that I was driving offensive coordinator Steve Ensminger crazy because of the number of plays I was making in practices. "Steve used to go insane when we were watching films and in coaching meetings," Clark said. "He'd say, 'Why isn't that kid playing for our defense right now? We must have some damned good linebackers if that kid isn't playing for us. He's in on every freaking play.'"

That was an exaggeration, but I was beginning to feel better about myself as the season progressed. Of course, many of my offensive teammates weren't actually patting me on the back for my physical transformation. To most of them, I became a nuisance, more annoying than a chirping cricket in the middle of the night. Frankly, I didn't care. After the way I had felt about myself when I first reported to A&M, I wasn't about to ease up—even when some of the offensive linemen began making threats in practice. I remember one day of practice, in particular, toward the end of the 1994 season when I shot through the gap and stuck our star tailback, Rodney Thomas, square in the chest. Rodney was the ultimate class guy, and he didn't say a word about it. It's football, after all, and Rodney just simply went back to the huddle. A couple of our linemen, on the other hand, had seen enough of me. "Hey freshman," one of them said to me, "if you want to play like that, you're going to pay the price. We're coming after you, you little brown-nosing punk."

Several of those guys also accused me of either overhearing the plays in the huddle or somehow knowing the plays in advance. I was guilty of the latter. With our offense back then it really wasn't too difficult to guess the plays in advance. It was usually as easy as assessing the down and distance and the personnel on the field. So, yeah, I guessed right most of the time. I was guessing right again on the next play in practice when one of our guards pulled to lead Thomas around the end. The guard was John Richard, who'd been particularly angered by my performance. He told me he was coming after me, and I was fully prepared when I coiled and then exploded into him. Richard, a senior at the time, went backwards and didn't immediately get up. So, the coaching staff moved the line of scrimmage up ten yards for the next play while the trainers tended to Richard.

Now several of the linemen were really ticked off. Jeff Jones, another senior, stepped in for Richard and said something to me like, "Okay, you son of a bitch, now you're really going down." But it was Jones who went down a few plays later—and stayed down after our violent collision. I think I knocked the wind out of him. It was nothing serious, but the line of scrimmage was once again moved up ten yards as the trainers tended to Jones. After that, no one really said too much to me about the way I was playing. In fact, I think I began to earn the respect of some of my teammates during the latter half of the 1994 season. On the other hand, I still wasn't feeling much love from Tommy Tuberville. For whatever reason, I don't think Tuberville liked me much. He may have even loathed me, as he had very little to do with me. That was a major problem as I looked toward the future. After all, Tuberville was my position coach and the ultimate decision maker on defense. So I was not necessarily brokenhearted when I first learned at the conclusion of the '94 season that Tuberville was leaving Texas A&M to become the head coach at Mississippi.

Prior to spring practices in 1995, R. C. Slocum announced the hiring of Phil Bennett as the new defensive coordinator and linebackers coach. Bennett, who had been the defensive coordinator at LSU before arriving at A&M, had played at A&M in

1976–77 and had served as a defensive coach for the Aggies from 1978 to 1981. I didn't know much about him at the time, but in hindsight, I could not have possibly picked a better teacher, technician, motivator, and friend than Coach Bennett. He had been a tough but undersized defensive end during his playing days at A&M, and he didn't seem fazed by my size at middle linebacker. In less than a year, I had gone from "Fat Dat" to, more or less, "Thin Nguyen." And at 5-foot-11, I was one of the shorter linebackers on the roster. None of that mattered to Coach Bennett, though. He didn't care who had the fastest forty-yard dash time or who looked best with his shirt off. Coach Bennett only cared about finding the eleven guys who could make the plays and putting them on the field. He had the same fire in his eyes that I had in mine, and we instantly hit it off.

In all my years of playing football, I would probably say that Mike Coleman, my defensive coordinator at Rockport-Fulton High School, had the biggest influence on me as a player. He really taught me about the finer points of the game. I knew I was a good athlete in high school, but Coleman, a former college quarterback, taught me how to read opposing offenses and anticipate what is most likely to happen. He taught me about tendencies, formations, and how to look for the depth of the running backs to determine who was going to get the ball. He also taught me to pay close attention to the "splits" between the offensive linemen, which would inevitably tell you whether it was going to be a run or pass. Coach Coleman gave me a major head start on my career in football, and Phil Bennett helped me take my game to the next level.

Coach Bennett was a no-nonsense, no-excuses kind of coach, who was quick to pat you on the back if you were working hard and doing what you were supposed to do and just as quick to provide some vocal motivation if you weren't. I think Coach Bennett took an instant liking to me because he didn't ever need to jump my case to get me going. After sulking my way through the first part of the 1994 two-a-days and then sitting out the entire '94 season, I didn't need any motivation to try to prove myself. I wanted to play, and I went through spring practices in 1995 under Bennett like a man on a mission. He took notice and soon took me under his wing. Bennett didn't tell me this at the time, but he later said that after that first spring, he knew I was going to be a player, and he believed I would eventually emerge as a starting inside linebacker. I also found out later from Coach Clark that, during a trip the coaches take each off-season, my name had come up several times in a positive light.

On one hand, I was feeling better and better about my chances of playing. But all I had to do to bring myself back to reality was to take a look at Trent Driver, who was one of the most purely athletic specimens I had ever seen. As much progress as I made toward the end of the 1994 season and during the spring of '95, I was still listed behind Driver in the post-spring depth chart that was printed in the media guide. Practically every time I looked at Driver I thought to myself, "I'm not even in this guy's league." Driver was so sleek that instead of a social security number he was initially assigned a vehicle ID number. Not only could he plug the gaps and make plays sideline to sideline, but I remember watching him after practice doing backward flips in pads. Then he did cartwheels without his hands ever touching the ground. His legs were so strong and he was so athletic that he would just fling himself into the air and land on his feet. If Trent had not been such a good-natured, easygoing guy, it would have been real easy to despise him. The rest of us sweated; Trent oozed athletic ability.

I stayed in College Station during the summer of 1995, going to summer school and continuing to work out every day with Rich and other teammates. I knew I would have a chance to play as a backup to Trent, so I continued to do everything I could to condition my body. During that summer, Rich and I would often work out three times a day. We would meet at the weight room in the morning, hook back up in the afternoons for our regular group session, and then meet back over at the Rec Center for an evening workout. All the countless hours of conditioning and training were paying off. Not only did I have a good spring, but Rich also turned plenty of heads, as well. They would put him at cornerback or safety, and Rich would make tackle after tackle and play after play. I remember one of the scholarship guys shaking his head after Rich made a play and saying, "Who the hell is this walk-on?" I said, "That's my partner."

As August rolled around and two-a-day practices grew nearer and nearer, the excitement really began to build. *The Sporting News* came out with its college football preview magazine, predicting the Aggies would win the national championship. *Playboy* magazine also picked A&M as No. 1 in its preseason poll, and most of our guys picked up that particular publication explicitly for the football articles. The Aggies had not won a national championship since 1939, but we seemed to have all the ingredients to make a serious run at college football's ultimate prize. We featured a Heisman Trophy candidate in Leeland McElroy, an experienced quarterback in Corey Pullig, some future NFL offensive linemen in Hunter Goodwin, Calvin Collins, Steve McKinney, and Chris Ruhman, and an outstanding newcomer at wide receiver in Albert Connell. Defensively, we were just flat-out loaded with All-American candidates such as Brandon Mitchell, Ray Mickens, and Reggie Brown and All–Southwest Conference candidates like Dennis Allen, Donovan Greer, Larry Walker, and Keith Mitchell.

We also entered the 1995 season with a twenty-nine-game unbeaten streak in the Southwest Conference and the nation's longest home winning streak. Even our schedule seemed to have national championship written all over it. A&M was often overlooked by the national media because the Southwest Conference was a lame duck league that was coming to an end at the conclusion of the 1995 season. The conference, composed then of eight teams from the state of Texas, was categorized as a regional league with no legitimate national powers. But even with a league schedule that featured perceived lightweights like SMU, TCU, Rice, and Houston, our non-conference schedule in 1995 was good enough to propel us into the national rankings. We opened the season with a home game against LSU and then traveled to Colorado to face the nationally ranked Buffaloes in the third game of the year. According to most of the preseason publications and the media analysts, if we could win at Colorado, there was no reason we couldn't at least play for it all. Even R. C. Slocum, who often leaned to the conservative side in his quotes to the media, seemed to be embracing the vision of the national championship. In the 1995 media guide, Slocum was quoted several times discussing the big picture. "When people start talking about teams who have a chance to win the national championship," Slocum said, "I want Texas A&M to be mentioned as one of those teams. . . . Sure, there is pressure. But that's the kind of pressure that helps you achieve great things." Slocum also said, "I believe this group wants even more than an unbeaten season and another Southwest Conference championship. Those are stepping stones to an even greater goal of a national championship. I sensed an even greater desire and work ethic at the end of the season last fall and through the off-season workouts and spring."

All that was true. We did sense that something special was building. I was also pleased when Slocum arranged for a picture of the Fiesta Bowl—site of the first-ever Bowl Coalition national championship game—to be placed on the wall as you entered our locker room. Slocum had to answer a bunch of questions from the media about putting that picture up, but I think it was appropriate. We wanted to play for it all, and we were intent on making the Fiesta Bowl our final destination for the season.

Once two-a-days started, the excitement only continued to build as it became apparent we featured speed and play makers at virtually every position. Driver was still clearly the starter in front of me as two-a-days came to an end, but Rich and I both began to realize that we were probably going to play a role on a team that should contend for the national championship. Rich continued to move up in the depth chart during two-a-days, moving into the playing rotation at strong safety behind Typail McMullen and Shun Horn. I vividly remember talking to Rich the week before the 1995 season opener against LSU, recalling just how far we had both come in the span of a year. We also discussed how excited we were about the possibility of playing against LSU before seventy thousand whooping, hollering fans at Kyle Field and a regional television audience on ABC. I figured, at the very least, that I would play a couple of series and ease my way into the big-time world of college football. Coach Bennett hinted at possibly even more playing time and there were several special teams opportunities, as well.

At least that was the plan until the end of practice on August 30—three days before the opener against the Tigers. We were running sprints to close the Wednesday practice when Trent suddenly went down on the grass practice fields. Driver possessed the muscular structure of a Rodin sculpture, but he apparently had ankles like the rest of us. Trent stepped in a hole while running sprints and turned his ankle. It wasn't a severe ankle sprain, but it was enough to keep him out of practice on Thursday and forced him to sit out of our walk-through on Friday. There was some speculation among media and fans that he could still start against the Tigers, but Coach Bennett put an end to that when he came to me and informed me that I would be starting against LSU. I was a stunned, excited, nervous, thrilled, and anxious combination of emotions as we checked in at the College Station Holiday Inn on the Friday before the game. I knew I was ready physically; I believed I could also play at this level. But was I ready mentally? Rich, who was always my roommate on the Friday night before games, spent hours talking about it with me in our hotel room, going over every possible assignment. He tried to convince me that I was, indeed, ready, and after we finally shut up and turned out the lights I spent some serious time praying for sleep and thanking God that at least it was an afternoon game and I didn't have to spend the entire day thinking about it.

I don't recall everything that was going through my head when the game finally kicked off, but I do recall my stomach was churning at full speed. I also remember running into the defensive huddle for my first play as an Aggie and being so excited that I could barely speak. I have a bit of a Vietnamese accent anyway, and when I get excited, it can be especially tough to decipher what I'm saying. That can be a rather significant problem when you are calling the defensive plays inside a packed stadium that is known for its noise level. I looked toward Coach Bennett on the sideline and excitedly called the formation and coverage. All the other ten players in the huddle looked at me as if I were speaking in Vietnamese. Reggie Brown, who is rather mild-mannered and soft-spoken, said the one thing that was probably on everybody's mind: "What the hell did you say? Slow it down, Dat, and say it again so that we can actually understand it."

Once I finally settled down and could audibly repeat the defensive signals, I quickly received a lesson in the speed of game day. On one of the first plays from scrimmage, LSU gave the ball to its all-everything tailback Kevin Faulk, who would go on to be a second-round draft pick in the NFL. I was supposed to sit in the B gap, but I didn't. The center pinned me to the inside and Faulk raced down the sideline for a 20- or 30-yard gain.

I remember Coach Bennett saying something the following Monday to the effect of: "Dang it, Dat, get across the center's face and maintain gap control." I was thinking, "Shoot, I'm going to lose my starting job because of that one play." It was an inauspicious beginning to my career, but I finally settled down and played pretty well, recording seven tackles in our 33–17 win. We started slowly as a team, as well. It was a scoreless tie at the end of the first quarter, and we had only a 5–0 lead late in the second before Leeland McElroy finally took control. McElroy had 359 all-purpose yards, and in the end, both Leeland's Heisman hopes and our national championship aspirations remained intact.

Trent Driver also played against the Tigers, and his ankle recovered somewhat in the two weeks before our next game against Tulsa. But Coach Bennett said he had seen enough from me to keep me in the starting lineup against the Golden Hurricane. I studied tape of Tulsa those entire two weeks and was completely prepared mentally and physically for that game. Then, on the second play of the game, I turned my ankle and had to go to the sidelines. It wasn't a severe sprain, but it kept me out of the game for quite some time and allowed Driver to earn the majority of the reps. At the conclusion of that game—which we won by a score of 52–9—Trent and I had each amassed three tackles. I was wondering if my starting days were coming to a close. But once again, Coach Bennett gave me a boost of confidence when he pointed out that I was more productive than Trent in the first two games. As we prepared for what could potentially be one of the biggest games in Texas A&M history, I felt firmly entrenched in my role as a starter in the middle of the Texas A&M defense. We were ranked No. 3 in the nation and were traveling to Boulder to face the No. 7 Buffaloes in a game that could have played a significant role in the national title picture.

I'm not claiming that we would have gone on to win the national championship if we had won that game against the Buffs.

After all, the 1995 Nebraska Cornhuskers were one of the most dominant teams in the history of college football. The Huskers went on to destroy Florida, 62–24, in the Bowl Coalition's national championship game at the Fiesta Bowl. Even if we had made it to the Fiesta Bowl, we might have been facing an uphill battle against Big Red. But if we had beaten the Buffaloes, we might have lived up to our preseason expectations. Instead, we went into Boulder and played like a team that was more scared to lose than driven to win. We had dreamed about this one game, read about it, fantasized about it, and pinned practically all our hopes on it. When we jumped to an early 7–0 lead, it appeared that we were well on our way to making a major statement to the nation. Keith Mitchell stripped Colorado quarterback Koy Detmer of the football early in the game, and David Maxwell pounced on it in the end zone to give us an early lead. Things continued to go our way a few minutes later when the extremely dangerous Detmer was forced out of the game with a knee injury on a play in which he wasn't even touched. But instead of going for the kill, we played far too cautiously. Colorado's backup quarterback, John Hessler, led the Buffs to 17 straight points to give the Buffs a 20–14 lead at the half. We managed to retake the lead in the third quarter, 21–20, but Colorado scored the final nine points of the game to win, 29–21.

To this day, it remains one of the most bitter and disappointing losses I've experienced. We had some tough calls from the officials—a Big Eight crew—and we made several very disheartening mistakes. I remember that one of Colorado's touchdowns came after an interception that went right through Albert Connell's hands, and a couple of other potential big pass plays were dropped by receivers. The Buffs also bottled up McElroy, popping him hard and often early in the game. He finished with only fifty-two rushing yards on twenty-three carries, which effectively ended his Heisman hopes. We didn't do the job defensively, either. We allowed a backup quarterback to beat us and allowed their young running back, Herchell Troutman, to run free. I truly believe we were the better team, but we didn't play like it. We played tight, and, as I've said, we played like a team that was merely trying not to lose.

In the post-game setting, Slocum stated the obvious to the media. Stuff like, "It was disappointing. . . . We didn't make the plays. . . . Half the teams in college football lost today." All that was true, but I have wondered from time to time if R. C. would have endeared himself much more to the players and fans if he had simply taken the responsibility. By no means am I insinuating that Slocum was the reason we lost. As players, we didn't get it done. But if a coach publicly accepts responsibility for a loss, it can be a rallying point for the team. When a coach like Bill Parcells steps up after a loss and says, "You can blame that one on me," it tends to make you want to play harder for that guy.

We were demoralized by the loss to Colorado, and we had two weeks to dwell on it as we prepared for our Southwest Conference opener at Texas Tech. When we arrived in Lubbock, we once again jumped to a quick 7–0 lead, but a couple of horrible calls kept Tech in the ball game. On the fifth play of the game, Keith Mitchell stripped Tech quarterback Zebbie Lethridge, causing a fumble that we recovered. Everybody in the stadium could clearly see that was what happened, but the officials said it wasn't a fumble. Then, late in the second half with the score tied at 7–7, Warrick Holdman stripped backup quarterback Sone Cavazos, and Reggie Brown scooped up the loose ball and ran twenty-nine yards for a touchdown. But the officials gathered again and decided that no fumble had occurred despite what the television replays clearly showed. As a result of the missed calls, we were tied with Tech, 7–7, late in the game. Although we hadn't moved the ball consistently all day and had already turned the ball over four times, we tried in desperation to take the ball the length of the field with less than a minute left. Instead, one of the truly great linebackers in the game, Zach Thomas, intercepted a pass and returned it twenty-three yards for the winning touchdown with thirty seconds left in the game.

In a matter of two weeks, we went from national title hopefuls to a team in utter disarray, and we continued our downward spiral the following week when SMU took a 10–0 lead into the locker room at halftime—at Kyle Field, no less—and then took a 17–13 lead with just fifty-six seconds left in the game. Aggie fans are famous for not booing, but the 59,573 fans who attended that game had every right to boo us right out of our stadium. Only a miraculous drive culminated by an even more remarkable touchdown pass and catch from Corey Pullig to Albert Connell with eight seconds left kept us from suffering the ultimate humiliation. Nevertheless, it was one of the most hollow victories I've ever experienced.

We finally righted the ship midway through the season, rolling to wins over Baylor, Houston, Rice, Middle Tennessee State, and TCU to set up a winner-take-all showdown with Texas for the SWC title and a berth in the Sugar Bowl. But as we had done so many times during the 1995 season, we seriously underachieved against the Longhorns. We turned the ball over six times and allowed a freshman running back named Ricky Williams to run wild on us, as Texas held on for a 16–6 win that ended our home winning streak at thirty-one games. In hindsight, it was probably a fittingly frustrating end to a terribly disappointing season. We were decent, but we should have been so much more, and I truly felt bad for seniors like Dennis Allen, Reggie Brown, Hunter Goodwin, Ray Mickens, and Corey Pullig. They deserved to go out on top—if not in the nation, then at least in the Southwest Conference. It was at least satisfying that those guys did go out with a bang, as we upset Michigan, 22–20, in the Alamo Bowl to finish the year at 9-3 and ranked fifteenth in the final national polls.

For me, finishing the year with a win over Michigan was also especially sweet. I had once envisioned myself playing for the maize and blue, and even after signing with A&M and reporting for two-a-days I had still thought about transferring to Michigan. But I realized in 1995 that I truly belonged at Texas A&M and had made the right decision by sticking around. I had made some extremely meaningful friendships with guys like Rich Coady and fellow freshmen like Dan Campbell, Toya Jones, Cameron Spikes, and Rex Tucker. That group would eventually form the foundation of my most memorable season in college. I had also proven I belonged at this level, starting every game and earning SWC Defensive Newcomer of the Year honors with ninety-four tackles for the season—the second highest total for a freshman in A&M history, behind Ed Simonini's ninety-eight stops in 1972. I even managed to return a kickoff for a touchdown, when I fielded an onside kick against Middle Tennessee State and looked up to see that no one was between me and the goal line. I kidded Leeland McElroy, Ray Mickens, and the rest of those guys who returned kicks and punts in 1995 that I was the only Aggie to return a kick for a touchdown that season. Of course, it's a good thing I only had to take it forty-six yards.

Perhaps most important from a football standpoint, I learned in 1995 to take labels in stride. In 1994, I had initially been labeled as a bust, and up until three days before the start of the '95 season, I was projected as a bench warmer on a national title contender. That didn't turn out to be the case in either category. Labels are great for canned goods, but you can probably shelve them when it comes to people. Whether you are being complimented or criticized, I realized that you simply cannot believe everything you read or hear. Not in football. Not in life. And especially not if you happen to be my guest at a traditional Vietnamese dinner. Poor Koby Hackradt didn't learn that until a few years later.

CHAPTER 8
Dance Hall Daze

Trust me: it's not nearly as bad as Becky makes it out to be. If you listen to her, you might be tempted to believe that I have so little rhythm I couldn't even play a radio. That's simply not true. I'm not holding out any long-term hopes that I will ever be asked to join a hip-hop boy band—although "Nguyen-Sync" has a nice ring to it—because of my musical talents and dance-floor moves. But hey, as I like to remind people, it was on a dance floor in 1995 that I first met my gorgeous wife. The short version of the story is that I left a major impression on her with my smooth, rhythmic moves and my feet that were so obviously made to move to the funk.

The long version of the story, though, is that the major impression I left on her was probably more negative than positive. After appeasing me on the dance floor for a few minutes, she pulled the old fake left, go right move. During our dance, she told me she needed to leave the floor to go to the bathroom. I naturally assumed she meant she was going to the bathroom *inside* the club. She apparently meant the one in her dorm room because she never came back. She left the building faster than a Barry Bonds home run headed for McCovey Cove. The next morning, while she was discussing her night out with her girlfriends, she casually informed them, "I danced with the biggest Chinese guy I've ever seen in my life."

Becky has become the love of my life, my soul mate, buddy, partner, and the answer to my prayers. I thank God for putting her in my life and making the life we have together possible. She is the wife of my dreams, and she is the best mother on the planet. I love her humor, wit, warmth, charm, intelligence, smile . . . everything about her. I also love thinking about our future together. But our past makes for some interesting imagery, as well. Becky is my most prized catch, but she was initially more difficult to corral than the Nebraska option in its prime. She gave me more slips than a water-slide park. There were polite brush-offs, "I just want to be friends" speeches, awkward times, down times, and times when she made it clear to me that it was over. It certainly didn't seem like one of those "meant to be" relation-ships. But from the night I first met her—and from the first mo-ment she ever "juked" me—I never really gave up on the idea of our being together.

If you could have seen it all unfold, you would have said I was a glutton for punishment. But I call it persistence. I saw the woman I wanted, and I never let go of that thought—even when I appeared to let her go. You know that silly old saying about how "if you love someone, let 'em go. If he or she comes back, you know it was meant to be." Well, there's probably some truth to that. It worked for me. In fact, it may have been my patience and persistence—even more than my best electric boogaloo dance moves—that finally won her heart.

Our first meeting took place during the summer of 1995 fol-lowing two-a-day practices of my redshirt freshman season. It was really late or really early—depending on your perspective—and I was with one of my friends from Rockport, Sam Spears. Sam and I had been doing a little unwinding as I celebrated the conclusion of two-a-days, and we decided to go into a dance club called Vertigo. As I previously mentioned, College Station is known for its conservatism. That one word typically describes the politics, culture, dress code, religious foundation, belief system, and just about everything else regarding the area's residents. But there is probably an eclectic clique within virtually every population base, and many of those folks were on display at Vertigo that night, jamming to the pulsating sounds of the techno beat that seemingly never ends. If you've ever been to a dance club like this, you've probably noticed that they only play one song. That one song happens to go on and on forever. Anyway, it was probably nearing 2:00 a.m. when I spotted Becky in the club. She was with one of her roommates, and although I'm not usually the aggressive type in a bar or club setting, I instantly knew I had to talk to this girl.

Becky has this cute, wholesome beauty and a smile that can practically melt an iceberg. So, I went to work on Sam, convincing him that we needed to go talk to those girls. I don't even remember how the conversation began, but after I found out her name, I mustered up the courage to ask her to dance. I found out she was a true freshman from a little town called Runge, which is about an hour south of San Antonio and smack in the middle of nowhere. I also detected right away that, despite her strikingly attractive looks, she didn't have a pretentious or arrogant bone in her body. I was taken with everything about her. I wouldn't necessarily say it was love at first sight, but it was at least captivation at first glance. After she told me she needed to go to the bathroom, I quickly began thinking of some smooth lines or interesting conversation topics to impress her when she came back.

As it turned out, I had about a year to think about it. When the house lights came on and the club began to close down, I finally came to the conclusion that Becky wasn't actually taking so long because she was primping in the bathroom to impress me; she was gone. I'm usually pretty good at remembering any face, and I was certain that she had a face I would not forget. Even on a campus with some forty-one thousand students at the time, I hoped I would eventually bump into her again. It didn't happen the rest of that semester, and it didn't happen during the spring or summer of 1996, either. Even though she made a major impression on me during our first meeting, I began dating someone else once again. My high school sweetheart from Rockport went to Sam Houston State University, and she and I continued an on-again, off-again relationship that began in high school and continued right on through my early college years. Of course, my top priority throughout the spring and summer of '96 was to focus on the upcoming season.

After our disappointing season in 1995, I was convinced we would rebound strongly in 1996. Even with the loss of some key performers like Corey Pullig and Leeland McElroy, our offense showed signs during the spring of '96 of being a high-powered unit. Quarterback Branndon Stewart, who transferred in from Tennessee after splitting time as a freshman with future NFL star Peyton Manning, looked impressive during the spring and in two-a-days. And the running back trio of Sirr Parker, D'Andre Hardeman, and Eric Bernard had stolen the show in the Alamo Bowl. They appeared to be capable of replacing McElroy, who left early for the NFL, without much of a drop-off. The only real concern was in the defensive secondary, where we were forced to replace starters Ray Mickens, Dennis Allen, and Typail McMullen. Cornerbacks Donovan Greer and Andre Williams also went through off-season knee surgeries.

Unfortunately, we opened the 1996 season with probably one

of the worst possible opponents for a young secondary: BYU. To make matters worse, we played them on their home turf in Provo, Utah. The Cougars were also coming off a disappointing season in 1995 when they had gone 7-4 and missed a bowl appearance for the first time in seventeen years. So, from the outside looking in, many college football fans assumed BYU was on a decline. Our school officials were probably of that same opinion when they agreed to play the Cougars in the 1996 Pigskin Classic. It seemed like a chance for us, the No. 12 team in the nation in the preseason polls, to play a "name" opponent on national television without the risk of actually playing a nationally ranked team. As it turned out, though, there was much more risk for us than anyone could have anticipated.

In watching the tapes of BYU from the previous season, I noticed that its quarterback, Steve Sarkisian, had seemed to get much better and much more comfortable as 1995 progressed. Still, no one could possibly have anticipated just how comfortable and in control he would be in the opening game of the 1996 season. There was plenty of hype surrounding the game, as we would be the first team from the newly formed Big 12 Conference to represent the league. Since the game was being played on August 24, every college football fan in the country would be tuned in for the first college game of the year.

What those college football fans witnessed was pure torture for us. Stewart, Parker, and Bernard looked good early on, as our offense piled up the yards and the points. We were leading 20–6 midway through the second quarter and had a chance to add to the lead when we fumbled a punt at our own 23. That turned the game around, as BYU scored the final 14 points of the half to tie it at 20–20 heading into the locker room. But even after that momentum swing, my man Rich Coady intercepted a Sarkisian pass late in the third quarter and returned it 64 yards to set up a touchdown that gave us a 34–26 lead heading into the fourth quarter. We were back in control. Or so it seemed. BYU tied the game early in the fourth quarter, and we took our last lead on a 52-yard field goal by Kyle Bryant with 1:27 left in the contest. But in just three plays, Sarkisian marched the Cougars down the field for what proved to be the game-winning score in a 41–37 loss. Our last gasp ended when we fumbled on the BYU 34 with about 20 seconds left in the game.

When the dust finally settled—and the celebrating BYU fans finally cleared the field with the goal post—the numbers were downright atrocious. Sarkisian had passed for 536 yards—the most ever yielded by an A&M defense. It was also the first time in the history of Texas A&M that we had scored as many as 37 points and failed to win a game. We boarded the plane back to Texas with a sober, sickening feeling. Perhaps the worst part of the entire trip was the realization that we had to wait three weeks until our next game. When you lose any game, especially a heartbreaker in the manner that we did where the Wrecking Crew was annihilated and humiliated, you want to get back on the field as quickly as possible to atone for your mistakes. But because LSU had backed out of a contract we had with them, and because we played such an early game against BYU, we had to wait three agonizingly long weeks before resuming our non-conference schedule at Southwestern Louisiana.

Three weeks is a long time for a layoff so early in the season, but it seemed more like three years. When we went back to work following our return from BYU, we basically went back to two-a-days. Any unity we had built as a team during our preseason workouts quickly dissolved as tempers flared and the intensity heightened. The offense was being praised in the press, while the defense was being scorned—a reversal of fortune from most of the previous scenarios in A&M history. The coaches seemed mad at us and at each other, and I think that it was during those three weeks when head coach R. C. Slocum and defensive coordinator Phil Bennett first began getting a little sideways with each other. Slocum had been a great defensive coordinator at A&M under Jackie Sherrill prior to becoming the head coach in 1989, and I think he still thought of himself as a defensive guru. He had a vision of what the Wrecking Crew should look like and how it should play. But with so many questions in the secondary, Coach Bennett couldn't afford to blitz and run stunts the way the Aggies had done when they had cornerbacks like Kevin Smith, Aaron Glenn, and Ray Mickens. I don't want to get into who was right or wrong, but we could sense that some animosity was building between Bennett and Slocum. We could also sense the frustration of everyone associated with that team. We worked so hard during those three weeks that we were physically and mentally exhausted by the time we left for Lafayette, Louisiana, on September 13, 1996.

Truthfully, it shouldn't have mattered how tired we were against Southwestern Louisiana, which was coming off a 55–14 loss at Florida. We were bigger, stronger, faster, and better than the Cajuns at virtually every position. USL featured a young quarterback, Jake Delhomme, who would eventually go on to NFL stardom, but he really didn't do anything to hurt us. We were simply bent on hurting ourselves. We probably went into that game still feeling sorry for ourselves and rather unfocused. Two of our star players, linebacker Keith Mitchell and wide receiver Albert Connell, were benched in the first half for violating team class attendance policies, and another young wide receiver, Aaron Oliver, was also suspended on the Monday before the game. Those things only added to the turmoil and the overall lack of focus that already existed following the loss to BYU and the torturous three weeks of practice that followed.

But none of those things seemed to matter when Donovan Greer intercepted Jake Delhomme's pass on the first play of the game and raced 27 yards to set up a touchdown that gave us a

7–0 lead with less than two minutes gone in the first quarter. From that point on, however, very little went our way. In front of the largest crowd (38,783) ever to watch a sporting event in Lafayette, we suffered perhaps the most humiliating defeat imaginable. We turned the ball over eight times, including three turnovers for touchdowns. We turned the ball over four times in the first quarter alone. Delhomme passed for only 128 yards, and USL managed just 248 yards of total offense and put together only one decent drive the entire game. It didn't matter, though. We turned the ball over in virtually every conceivable way and were pinned with a demoralizing, 29–22 loss to a team that had no business staying on the same field with us. For the second consecutive game, we watched as an opposing crowd stormed the field after a game and tore down a goal post.

If the loss to BYU was tough to take, the loss to USL was downright unbearable. While you could sense the tension on the field and in the locker room after our first loss, you could cut it with a knife following the loss to the Cajuns. I remember Coach Bennett pulling me to the side during the week after the trip to USL and giving me a personal pep talk. He told me he was proud of the way I had been playing and told me that I had a future at the next level. It was the first time anyone had ever even mentioned the NFL to me, and I was really wondering why he was bringing it up now. Then he told me that he didn't expect to be around the next season. That didn't come as much of a shock to me considering how tense the mood was among the coaching staff. But I was extremely honored that Coach Bennett thought enough of me that he made it a point to pull me aside. I had seventeen tackles in the loss to USL, and he said, "Average guys don't make seventeen tackles no matter who they are playing against. You can be one of the best linebackers in the country, and you can play at the next level if you keep working and improving."

After we were leveled by the Cajuns, "the next level" seemed like a pipedream to me. One of the only things that made that 1996 season bearable for me was my relationship with Coach Bennett and his family. Coach Bennett could be as tough as nails, but he also cared deeply about his players and would do anything he could to help them develop as football players and people. He could knock you down if you got too big for your britches, but he was also just as likely to build you back up if you were down in the dumps. He also obviously knew what he was doing—he was named the 1995 Defensive Coordinator of the year by the *American Football Quarterly*. And his wife, Nancy, became almost like a second mom to me during 1995 and 1996. Coach Bennett would occasionally invite some of the players over to his house for skinless fried chicken, and it was in those settings where I truly fell in love with the Bennett family. Nancy and Coach Bennett had met while they were students at Texas A&M in the late 1970s, and they formed the perfect complement to each other. He was hard-charging, intense, and driven for perfection; she was soft-hearted, compassionate, and kept everything in perspective. As I watched Nancy support her husband and care for the couple's two amazing children, Sam and Maddi, I probably began to formulate some visions in my own mind of what I was looking for in my ideal mate.

While Coach Bennett was a mentor on the field, Nancy became a confidante off of it. Nancy's personality was as radiant as a jewelry store's diamond display case. She and I had many discussions about school, family, faith, dating, and life in general. When I felt the need to talk to someone about personal issues, I often gave Nancy a call. She became an extremely special friend, and I became so enamored with the Bennett kids that I practically adopted Sam and Maddi as my nephew and niece.

But following our 0-2 start and Coach Bennett's talk with me,

I began to realize that the Bennett family might not be around College Station much longer unless we made a dramatic turnaround on the field. After starting the season ranked No. 12 in the preseason polls, we plummeted to No. 25 following the loss to BYU, and after losing to USL, we dropped out of the polls for the first time since 1991. A&M had been in the polls for 109 straight weeks, but that streak came crashing to a halt after our collapse in Lafayette. We obviously still had ten games left to play, but our psyche was as fragile as an eggshell, and our chemistry was as volatile as the smoking flask of a mad scientist.

Unfortunately, nobody really stepped up to assume control of our floundering ship. I think virtually every good college team needs some strong, vocal leadership from its seniors. We had some good guys and great players in our senior class in 1996, as evidenced by the fact that seven of our eleven seniors went on to play in the NFL. But standout players like Brandon Mitchell, Eddie Jasper, and Pat Williams were more soft-spoken than outspoken. And our outstanding outside linebacker, Keith Mitchell, was more of a playmaker than a locker room spokesman. Besides, Keith and Slocum didn't see eye-to-eye on several things, and you could sense some growing tension between them. Despite being an incredibly productive sack specialist and an All-American, Mitchell went undrafted following the '96 season. Fortunately, Keith went on to an outstanding pro career, signing a free agent contract with New Orleans and eventually becoming a Pro Bowl player. But it was truly a shame that he was not drafted coming out of A&M, just one result of the underlying turmoil we had in 1996.

We finally were able to take out our frustrations on an opponent when we beat North Texas, 55–0, in the third game of the season. That set up a showdown with Colorado, which had ruined our 1995 season, in the first Big 12 game ever to be played at Kyle Field. We fumbled the opening kickoff, and thirteen seconds into the game, the Buffs led 7–0. In the end, the rematch was no match, as Colorado cruised to a 24–10 win. As a result, we were 1-3 and completely off the national radar.

In our next two games, we hammered Louisiana Tech and slipped past Iowa State to move back up to .500. Then after falling behind Kansas State 20–3 at the half on October 19, we came storming back to pull within 3 points, at 23–20, late in the fourth quarter. We had a chance to win the game, as Branndon Stewart hit Albert Connell on a big pass at the KSU 17, but—fittingly for the season—we fumbled and lost by 3. It was a bitter pill to swallow, and we would receive yet another dose of that bitter medicine the following week when we built a 10–6 lead over Texas Tech and were driving deep in Red Raiders territory late in the third quarter. Once again, we found a way to lose, fumbling at the Tech seven and then allowing fullback Sammie Morris to take a short pass for an eighty-one-yard touchdown. One of our defensive backs slipped down on the play, and at 3-5 overall and 1-3 in the Big 12, we could all sense our season slipping away.

I was at my wit's end, and following our loss to Tech, I was in need of a serious mood alteration. One of my childhood friends from Rockport, Stephen Levy, was a student at Texas Tech and had come in for the game with one of his college friends. They joined me and my roommates, Smith Nguyen and Chau Ngo, at my apartment the night following the loss to Tech, and we decided to have a few beers and unwind. It's my policy—now, as well as back then—never to drink beer or any alcoholic beverage during the season. I celebrated my twenty-first birthday by raising iced tea toasts. I don't ever advocate drowning your sorrows in beer. But with our season spiraling out of control, it didn't take much arm-twisting on my friends' part to convince me that a couple of cold beers might do me some good. We then learned of a party that was being thrown a couple of sections down from my apartment. Parties in college apartment complexes are held all the time, but when we heard it was a big birthday bash given by four girls who also lived in the complex, it piqued our interest. So we walked over to the party, and people were literally wall-to-wall inside the apartment and lined up and down the staircase. With so many people inside and out, it would have been easy to overlook anyone at the party, but after just a few minutes of mingling through the crowd, I noticed a beautiful young woman who looked remarkably familiar to me. I didn't place her face right away, but after a couple of minutes, I realized it was none other than the beautiful Rebekah L. Foster, otherwise known as Becky.

Isn't it amazing how God works? Here I was in the dumps, feeling a little sorry for myself because our season was going south, and when I feel like I've hit rock bottom, God shows me that the woman of my dreams is living just a couple of doors down from my own apartment. Obviously, I didn't know at the time that I would eventually share my life with this woman, but the mere sight of her beaming smile and beautiful face that night did lift my spirits. I noticed at the party that she was with her boyfriend, but I still made it a point to talk to her and reintroduce myself. When I walked up to her and invaded her space, she looked at me with one of those, "Who are you?" looks. I then reminded her of our dance together more than a year earlier and made a joke about her getting lost on the way back from the bathroom to the dance floor. She giggled in her cute, trademark way, and after a short conversation, we parted ways. I told her I lived a couple of units down, and she mentioned that she hoped to bump into me again.

I made sure that she did. Over the next few months, I spent much of my time away from the football field and classroom in my mini-backyard at the Treehouse Apartments. Each of the first-floor apartments featured a tiny backyard area that was

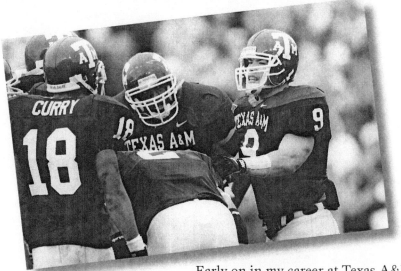

Early on in my career at Texas A&M, my teammates had to strain to hear what I was saying in the huddle. Photo courtesy *12th Man Magazine*

I scored a touchdown on this fumble recovery against Kansas State in 1996. But, fittingly for the season, it was called back. Photo courtesy *12th Man Magazine*

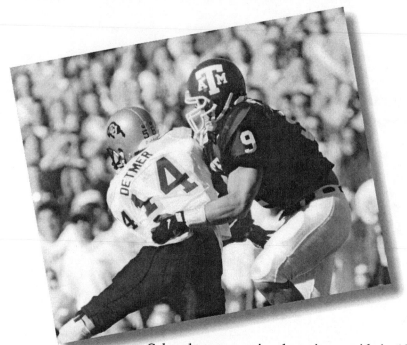

Colorado was a major thorn in our side in 1995 and again here in '96. Payback was sweet in 1997, though. Photo courtesy *12th Man Magazine*

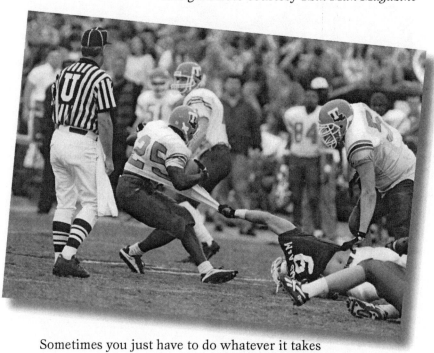

Sometimes you just have to do whatever it takes to bring down a ball carrier. Photo courtesy *12th Man Magazine*

After we wrapped up the Big 12 South title in 1998, I tossed my helmet into the air and began looking for folks to hug. Aaron Oliver was the "lucky" recipient here. Photo courtesy *12th Man Magazine*

This 1997 game against North Texas was actually my first opportunity ever to play in Texas Stadium. Photo courtesy *12th Man Magazine*

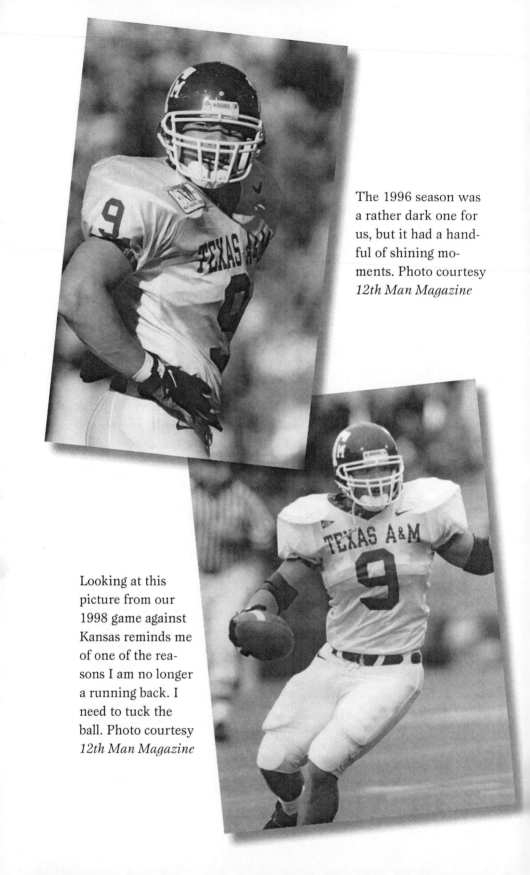

The 1996 season was a rather dark one for us, but it had a handful of shining moments. Photo courtesy *12th Man Magazine*

Looking at this picture from our 1998 game against Kansas reminds me of one of the reasons I am no longer a running back. I need to tuck the ball. Photo courtesy *12th Man Magazine*

Opening the 1998 season against a team like Florida State helped us in the long haul. We lost that game, but we knew we could hang with the best of the best. Photo courtesy *12th Man Magazine*

We were Number 1—at least in the Big 12—in 1998.
This is just my friendly reminder to our visitors from Missouri.
Photo courtesy *12th Man Magazine*

Man, do I ever look young here. Now, I'm just young at heart. Photo courtesy *12th Man Magazine*

I sometimes like to joke around with my friends about this billboard on Highway 35 in Rockport, but it really is a big honor for me. Photo by Rusty Burson

There was some foreshadowing going on in this picture of me winning the Lombardi Award. Pictured along with finalists Aaron Gibson of Wisconsin *(far left)* and Ohio State's Andy Katzenmoyer *(far right)* are former Dallas Cowboys quarterback Roger Staubach and Dallas Cowboys radio announcer Brad Sham. Photo courtesy *12th Man Magazine*

My parents, shown here at the Lombardi Award presentation, initially thought I was pulling their leg when I told them that coaches like R. C. Slocum were willing to give me a college scholarship because of my abilities on the football field. Photo courtesy *12th Man Magazine*

Two of my coaching mentors, former A&M coach R. C. Slocum *(left)*
and my junior high basketball and football coach, Cliff Davis. I asked
both Slocum and Davis to be present at Kyle Field when I was unable
to be at my induction into the A&M Athletics Hall of Fame. Photo
courtesy *12th Man Magazine*

only big enough for a barbecue grill, a cooler, and a couple of lounge chairs. But in our backyard, we had a small, artificial turf putting green that I spent a considerable amount of time on each day. Coincidentally, I just happened to be practicing my putting each day about the same time Becky arrived home from class and made her way from the parking lot to her apartment. We had so many conversations over the six-foot fence that she began calling me Mr. Wilson—a reference to Tim Allen's neighbor on the television sitcom *Home Improvement.* Throughout the duration of the television show, you never really saw Wilson's entire face; mostly you saw only the top of his face, from the nose up, peering over the fence. That's how the friendship between Becky and me first began to develop, and it really was only a friendship at first. But as I began to see her more and more and began to get to know her, I admit that my desire to be more than friends increased.

From the night that I ran into her again at the party, Becky began to brighten up my life. I loved the way she talked, the way she laughed, and her remarkable sense of humor. She looked awesome when she was dressed up to go out on a Friday or Saturday night, but she even looked beautiful in baggy sweatpants and a T-shirt. For that matter, she also looked beautiful the day she went to class with two different shoes on. In her haste to make it to class on time, she went out the door with one brown and one black shoe. I had fun with that one as we went to class. She told me that no one else had noticed, but I did. I noticed virtually everything about her. My admiration for her continued to grow over the next few months as I noticed that she went to church every Sunday morning. Attending church service is very important to me, and I was impressed that it was also a priority in her life.

Actually, I was impressed with just about everything about her, and I was impressed with how she made me feel when I was around her. As a matter of fact, everything started going better after I ran into Becky again at the party. We won our next three games, beating Oklahoma State, Baylor, and Oklahoma to improve to 6-5 on the season and 4-3 in the Big 12. We had to come back from halftime deficits in each of those three wins, but our winning streak put us in position to go to a bowl game if we could win the season finale against Texas. Unfortunately, beating the Longhorns in Austin would prove to be more than we could handle. Texas jumped up on us 10–0 in the first quarter, but we came back to cut it to 10–9 in the second quarter. It was all downhill from there. Ricky Williams went nuts in the second half, rushing for 145 yards, and the Horns scored 41 straight points. Midway through the fourth quarter, we were down 51–9. Sirr Parker returned the ensuing kickoff 100 yards for a touchdown to make it 51–15, but it was far too little, far too late to make a significant difference. We started the season against BYU by giving up the most passing yards an A&M defense had ever surrendered, and we finished the year by giving up 594 yards against Texas, the most allowed by an A&M team since 1970.

We finished the year 6-6, unranked and at home for the bowl season for the first time since 1984 (excluding the probation years of 1988 and 1994). The sickening part of being home for the holidays was that we were talented enough to be in a bowl game. It also was tough to watch Texas go on to beat Nebraska in the inaugural Big 12 title game, grabbing national headlines for their upset of the Huskers.

I ended the season with 146 tackles, finishing second in the Big 12 behind Colorado's Ryan Black. I might have ended up with more if not for a ruptured bursa sac in my right knee throughout much of the season. During a five- or six-game stretch through the middle of the season, my knee would swell up to the size of an orange on some days and a cantaloupe on other days. It didn't hurt that much, but the swelling did limit my mobility. You probably could have irrigated a small farm with the amount of fluid they drained from my knee that year. But despite the swelling, I earned some All-Big 12 honors in '96 and began being compared to one of the great linebackers in A&M's history, Ed Simonini. I was born the same year Simonini finished his outstanding college career at A&M in 1975, so I couldn't say I was floored by the comparison. I was taken aback, however, when former Baylor coach Grant Teaff said that I reminded him a little of Mike Singletary in terms of my size and knack for being around the football. When I read that in an article, I was stunned and even a little embarrassed. Mike Singletary is one of the greatest middle linebackers in the history of the game. Even to be mentioned in the same sentence with him was eye-opening.

Despite some of the individual honors and accolades I received, I was pretty disgusted by the 1996 season. The frustration was made even worse by the firing of Phil Bennett at the end of the year. Slocum also fired two other coaches—offensive coordinator Steve Ensminger and receivers coach Les Koenning—and a third coach, Mike Sherman, left for the NFL's Green Bay Packers. It obviously turned out to be a good move for Coach Sherman, who would go on to become the head coach and general manager of the Packers. When all was said and done, we lost nearly as many assistant coaches (four) as seniors (eleven). You don't go through a season with that much frustration and that much disappointment without expecting some changes. But seeing Coach Bennett leave, along with Nancy and their two children, was tough to take. I really felt I had lost some of my best friends when the Bennetts left town.

Here again, the most frustrating part of watching Coach Bennett leave was that it should have been so much different. He was the Defensive Coordinator of the Year in 1995, and he was fired in 1996. He didn't forget how to coach in a one-year span.

It was a lack of production from the players and an overall lack of chemistry among the players and staff. I looked around on the sidelines during our humiliating loss to Texas at the end of the season and actually saw some of our guys laughing, smiling, and cutting up. The Texas fans were chanting "Pooooor Aggies, Pooooor Aggies," and some of our guys obviously didn't care enough even to pretend that it bothered them. It certainly bothered me, and it continued to bother me throughout the rest of the off-season. I felt embarrassed for our fans, our former players, and our students. Going 6-6 with our kind of talent was inexcusable. Losing to Southwestern Louisiana, dropping three games at Kyle Field, and being blown out by Texas were simply unacceptable outcomes. I vowed to myself at the end of that season that I would do everything possible to make sure we did not go through another year like that. I've never been an outspoken guy, and it's not really in my personality to be one of the spokesmen of the team. But when guys like Steve McKinney and Dan Campbell stepped forward in the off-season of 1997 and basically laid down the law to the rest of the team, presenting an ultimatum to either jump on the bandwagon or get lost, I was one of the first ones to hop aboard.

Atoning for the frustration of the 1996 season basically consumed me. That . . . and the thought of spending time with one Becky Foster. Following the loss to Texas on the day after Thanksgiving, I received a little emotional pick-me-up when Becky invited me over to her apartment to decorate their Christmas tree. Through our "fence" conversations, I had found out that she and her boyfriend from high school were much like me and my girlfriend from high school: on again, off again. Becky and I were still just friends, but I was growing more and more attracted to her. Then, when we all came back to begin the spring semester in 1997, we began going out in group settings. Her friends and my friends would meet from time to time at a club or at my apartment just to hang out and talk. Rich Coady was constantly making fun of me because of the number of parties I was hosting. I would invite friends over several nights a week and then call Becky to tell her I was having a party. In all honesty, the parties were designed for the sole purpose of spending more time with Becky. I also learned during these times that she had finally called it off with her high school sweetheart. I tried to act sympathetic, but deep-down, I was delighted.

I didn't want to rush things, and I didn't want to force the issue. But I was looking for the opportune time to let her know that I wanted to be more than friends. Valentine's Day in 1997 appeared to be that time. Since both of us had finally broken up with our high school sweethearts, I knew Becky would be dateless on the big day. So, I called her, and I casually asked her if she wanted to go to dinner. Her response left me as dumbfounded as our defense against BYU. She said, "No, thanks." She said it very nicely, but she still said no. We talked a few minutes on the phone and than we hung up. I was thinking to myself, "It's Valentine's Day, for Cupid's sake. If she won't go out with me on Valentine's Day, then when will she ever go out with me?" I paced the floor of my apartment for about an hour and began to contemplate my next move. I had already determined that there definitely would be a next move.

Here's the one thing you count on about me: I don't give up easily. You can call it persistence, determination, resolve, fortitude, or even just plain hardheadedness. The bottom line is that in my own vocabulary, *quit* is the worst of the four-letter words. I'm certain I received that quality from my parents, who made the decision in Vietnam that they would rather die trying to fulfill their dreams than ever give up on them. In this particular case, Becky Foster was certainly part of my dream scenario. So, about an hour after she had turned down my first dinner offer because she thought I was only feeling sorry for her because she was alone on Valentine's Day, I called her back and asked her out again. Once again, she said, "No, that's okay; don't worry about me."

Here again, I realize that most guys probably would have gotten the message after two "no, thank you" replies. But hey, it's not "one, two strikes you're out at the ol' ballgame." So, even after two rejections, I began thinking of my next move. I called Rich Coady and Koby Hackradt—I knew those guys wouldn't be busy on Valentine's Day—and told them I needed them to get over to my place right away because we needed to go out. After a little arm-twisting, they obliged, knowing full well that this probably involved yet another scheme of mine to spend time with Becky. Then I called Becky back for a third time and asked her to go out once again. Before she could answer, I told her that it wasn't a date; we were going out as a group. She finally agreed, and I did a little celebration dance when I hung up the phone. After all, we were officially going out on Valentine's Day. Just me and Becky . . . and my obscure wingmen. When we had previously hooked up to go out as a group, it was usually a combination of Becky's friends and my friends. This time, it was just the four of us, and like good little wingmen, Rich and Koby made themselves scarce once we arrived at the Barracuda Bar. We talked and talked until Rich and Koby finally said they were ready to go. They dropped Becky and me off at the Treehouse Apartments, and thanks to a couple of drinks and perhaps the magic of Valentine's Day, we had our first kiss when I walked her to her apartment door.

I'd love to tell you that I completely swept her off her feet with that first kiss and that from that point on, we lived in courtship bliss right up until our marriage in March of 2001. But the reality is that we were in for some more turbulent times ahead. We dated for several months, and I loved every minute of it. But I could sense that Becky still wasn't completely sure she wanted to be in a serious relationship with me. We had become such good friends that, on the one hand, we were completely at ease with each other. We were also such good friends that Becky still felt a little strange calling me her boyfriend. When she moved out of the Treehouse apartment complex in May of 1997 to a place in Bryan, I sent her a dozen roses because our relationship had begun at the Treehouse. But by late July or early August Becky did her best Steve Sarkisian/Koy Detmer impression, throwing a bomb on me one day when I went to visit her. She said she needed time to be alone; she said she didn't think it was working out between us in the manner she had hoped; and she said our dating relationship was over.

I've been hit hard on the football field more times than I can possibly recall. But this bombshell news hit me like a Mack truck. I had found the woman of my dreams, and she had decided it was better to put an end to this before we ended up getting hurt. I wanted to say, "I'm already hurt." I didn't. I am one of those people who truly believes that everything happens for a reason. In a previous relationship I had tried to force the issue too hard when things appeared to be coming to an end. I learned my lesson from that relationship. So, I told Becky that I wished her only the best, and that I truly had enjoyed getting to know her and spending the time we did together. I gave her a hug and left with one reminder: She knew how to reach me if she ever wanted to talk again. I wasn't quitting or giving up on us, but I was resigned to the fact that it might be over. I had tried to win her over with my charm, wit, and personality. I had spent so much time on that putting green just waiting for her that I should have been applying for my PGA card. I had tried to arrange meetings, parties, group outings, and everything else just to spend time with her or see her. I had gone to coffee shops with her and pretended that I was drinking coffee—even though I didn't like coffee at the time—just to be around her. I had even tried to impress her with my dancing shoes. But now I decided it was probably in my best interest to focus 100 percent of my energy on winning games instead of winning one woman's heart. As it turned out, that mindset helped make 1997 a very memorable year for me—both on the field and off.

CHAPTER 9
Clock Management

ONCE A FOOTBALL SEASON BEGINS, eliminating as many distractions as possible ranks high among my top priorities. During the off-season, I thoroughly enjoy working with charitable organizations, donating time to my church, and making public appearances. I also enjoy traveling, spending time with extended family members, and simply living a more relaxed lifestyle. In my profession, you must bust your butt to stay in shape all twelve months a year, but from late January to March, my time is often a little more flexible, and my day-to-day pace resembles a jog more than a sprint.

When the season begins, however, I switch to full-throttle. To perform at a peak level against some of the most talented athletes on the planet, it's essential to prioritize and eliminate time drainers. I don't play golf during the season; I don't watch movies; I don't play video games; and I don't even particularly like to do any media interviews. Unlike some professional athletes, I don't have an axe to grind with the media, and I realize it would probably be in my best interest from a publicity standpoint to spend more time in front of the microphones. But quite honestly, when I'm at the practice facility, I'd much rather study the next opponent in the film room than be filmed. Basically, if it doesn't involve my faith, my family, or my football preparations, it's a low priority once the season starts.

My typical day during the season begins with waking up early and spending a little quiet time in prayer and in reading. Then, I'll brush my teeth, throw on a T-shirt and shorts, and head out the door for meetings, practice, conditioning, and film study. Most of the time, I don't even bother combing my hair before heading to work. What's the point in primping if I'm going to be wearing a helmet at my "office?" At least during the season, even brushing my own hair falls into the "low priority" category. Once I get home, I spend as much family time as possible before ending the day with more film study of the next opponent. Then it's time to get to bed as early as possible. I don't mind staying up late on occasion during the off-season, but in this profession, I know I'd better be rested and ready for the next day.

That's my typical in-season routine. It was obviously a little different when I was back at Texas A&M and was also trying to balance my academic calendar with my football priorities. I was the first person in my family to graduate from college, earning a degree in agricultural development even before playing my senior season. But even in college, I tried to eliminate as many distractions as possible during the season, which meant saying no to many requests for public appearances and passing up potential sleep inhibitors. Of course, there's usually an exception to any rule, and occasionally making time for so-called distractions or losing a little sleep every once in a while can make life much more fulfilling. Even during the football season.

For example, there was the time at Texas A&M when John Thornton, who was then the assistant athletic director of student services, contacted me about a request he had received from a local elementary school. A fifth-grade teacher at Mary Branch Elementary School in Bryan, Jennifer Paderas, was familiar with my story. She was an A&M graduate and a football season-ticket holder, and she knew my family had escaped from Vietnam. So, when a Vietnamese student named Quang Pham showed up in her class with almost no knowledge of the English language, Paderas gave John Thornton a call to see if I could come by the school and spend some time with Quang. It was during the football season, so Thornton was reluctant to promise anything. When I heard about this particular case, however, I knew it was something I needed and wanted to do.

I recalled the stories of my oldest brother, Ho, attending classes with kindergarteners when he was eleven because he didn't speak English, and I also recalled my own struggles. I attended American public schools throughout my life, but I still labored in classroom settings during my early days at Texas A&M while trying to keep up with professors during lectures and in my reading and writing. Growing up in a home where my parents spoke only Vietnamese probably put me at a little disadvantage in the college classroom, so I had to work a little harder than some of my Aggie classmates in terms of my English comprehension. When I heard about an opportunity to help a youngster struggling with some of the same issues, I was excited about possibly being able to ease some of his concerns.

I showed up at the school, and some of the other English-speaking kids came running up to me for an autograph. Quang didn't initially have any idea who I was, but when I began speaking to him in a language he could understand, his face lit up. I told him I understood how hard this transition was, and I told him how important it was to stick to it and work through the difficulties. We spent some time together, and he made such an impression on me that I told Jennifer Paderas I would see her at the same time next week. She was shocked. She had asked only that I come by that one time, but I made it a point to go by the school once a week throughout the fall to work with Quang on his language skills. I was delighted to learn that during the few weeks I spent working with him, his reading ability improved from a pre-kindergarten level to a second-grade level. I was even more touched when Paderas told me that after my first visit with Quang, he came back the next day with a new hairstyle. He walked into the classroom and said, "Ms. Paderas, Ms. Paderas, look, hair like Dat."

This was obviously back in the day when I viewed combing my hair as a higher priority. Nowadays, "hair like Dat" could often be described as "bed head." But that's not the issue. The point here is that the weekly time we spent together made a huge difference in his confidence, his outlook on school and his desire to learn a new language. It cost me a little afternoon study and relaxation time, forcing me to stay up a little later to catch up with my football film work and classroom studies. Was it worth it? Absolutely.

That was some of the best sleep I've ever missed. The very best sleep I ever passed up, however, came during two-a-days in 1997. If you've ever been through high school or college two-a-day practices you know how much your body craves and covets sleep. If you haven't been through two-a-day practices, you can experience what it's like by taking an August jog from Dallas to Fort Worth along Interstate 30 while wearing ski pants and a leather jacket. To simulate the contact, tackle a few oncoming motorcycles along the way. Do the same thing coming back, and you'll have an idea of what it's like to go through one day of it. Two-a-day practices are a torturous survival test, where weaknesses are exposed and iron wills are shaped. As I recall quite clearly, the 1997 two-a-day practices were the toughest of my first four years at A&M. After going 6-6 the season before, we all had something to prove. Our coaching staff, which included new defensive coordinator Mike Hankwitz, new offensive coordinator Steve Marshall, new quarterbacks coach Ray Dorr, and new receivers coach Steve Kragthorpe, pushed us hard. More important, we pushed ourselves harder than ever before.

Dan Campbell has told me the story about how he and Steve McKinney went to Dallas to watch McKinney's younger brother, Seth, play in a high school playoff game following our 1996 loss to Texas. During that high school game, Campbell and McKinney—two outspoken, natural leaders—decided that 1997 was going to be different, and that the '97 team was going to be "their team." That was a turning point for the A&M program. As Campbell said, "Steve and I got our frustrations out on the table. I told him, 'Steve, I've never been so frustrated in my whole life. Football wasn't fun for me last year.' He felt the same way. We were both full of rage, and we made a vow to do whatever it took not to let 1996 happen again. We weren't going to get embarrassed again, we were going to play until the very end of every stinkin' game, and we were going to work our butts off. That's where it began for us. We already had guys who were willing to pay that price. But they just needed some internal leaders to take charge." That's the cleaned-up, edited version of Campbell's story. But that's also exactly what happened. Some guys may have resented it, but I loved it. We needed take-charge, outspoken leaders to provide some discipline, some accountability, and even some intimidation. When Campbell and McKinney laid down the laws—which covered such things as practice intensity, workout intensity, and consequences for failing to meet those intensity standards—some of the guys were probably a little unnerved. Campbell and McKinney were already a little crazy, and now they were enraged. I don't think anyone was really sure exactly what they meant when they said they would personally do "whatever it took" to ensure that everybody was on the same page. I am certain, though, that nobody wanted to find out about the consequences.

So, whether it was out of personal pride, frustration from the year before, or fear of Campbell and McKinney, we worked our butts off during the 1997 two-a-days. We were unranked in most of the preseason magazines and polls, and the only real attention we received from the national media was for our non-conference schedule. Reporters ripped us for opening the season against Sam Houston State, Southwestern Louisiana, and North Texas. Of course, they usually failed to mention that the reason we played those three schools was because Auburn and LSU had backed out of contracts to play us. Nevertheless, we had plenty of motivational fuel to fill our tanks during two-a-days. For me personally, the added intensity during practices and the complete exhaustion at the end of the day were more of a blessing than a nightmare. We were working so hard that I didn't really have the time or the energy to dwell on how much I was hurting emotionally because of Becky's decision to break off our relationship. I missed seeing her; I missed holding her; and most of all, I missed talking to her. Whether it was face-to-face or on the phone, we had often spent hours talking to each other about virtually nothing during our courtship and early dating days. I missed her voice.

I was so tired during two-a-days that when my head hit the pillow, I was out. At the end of a long day, I didn't have to debate about whether I should call her or not. I told myself that she needed her space, and I needed my sleep. It had been at least two weeks since she called it off with me when the phone rang late one evening at my apartment. In a sleepy daze, I picked it up. It was Becky. Little did I know that she had been waiting by the phone every evening for two weeks in hopes I would call. When I didn't, she began to realize I meant more to her than simply being a "rebound" following her previous relationship. We talked that night for three or four hours, catching up on all the things we had missed during the previous two weeks. I was exhausted when we finally hung up about 1:00 or 2:00 in the morning, but I didn't care—at least until the next morning. I was one tired pup during practices the following day, but I was also excited about the possibility of reuniting with Becky. Of course, I still didn't want to appear overanxious. While I wanted to call her as soon as I got home from the evening practice, I didn't. Instead, she called me again. This time, we probably talked until 2:00 or 3:00 in the morning. I was again dead tired the next day for practice, but it was worth it. After that second long conversation, Becky and I were once again an "item." This time, we both knew just how much we meant to each other. There would be no more breaks or awkward times, which made the rest of my time at Texas A&M feel more complete, more enjoyable, and far more fun.

We began dating seriously during the 1997 season. But we were anything but serious in terms of how we acted around each other. Then and now, Becky and I are like two little kids trapped in grown-up bodies when we're together. Even when we first started dating and were supposedly trying to impress each other, we were just flat-out goofy. Every Sunday after church, we would go to the Olive Garden restaurant in College Station and spend hours laughing at each other. Inevitably, one or both of us would wind up balancing spoons on our noses and laughing hysterically. I don't know why that trick never gets old for us, but it doesn't. We also have a great time poking fun at each other and just flirting with each other. For example, she says we don't go out dancing anymore because I don't have any rhythm. I say we don't go out dancing any more because it is so much more fun simply to turn on the music in our home and let Becky perform her most sensuous moves for me. The truth is probably that it's just too hard to balance spoons on your noses when you're on a crowded dance floor.

We are so compatible with each other that we don't need to go out dancing, to go to movies, to go bowling, or to go anywhere else to enjoy each other. We'll do some of those things on occasion, but mostly, we just enjoy each other's company. And quite frankly, we're more entertained by each other than by watching a movie or going out. At A&M our typical date would consist of going out to eat and, after drawing stares and scorn from the rest of the restaurant because of our laughing outbursts, taking a drive around town or around a neighborhood. We'd just drive around and talk with the cell phones off and the radio on. Of course, we usually received a few more stares, especially when we'd drive through a neighborhood. Becky still listens to country music, and I still listen to Vietnamese music. So, as kind of a halfway point, we would often listen to rap music in the car together. When a Vietnamese guy and a white girl are driving around listening to rap music with the windows rolled down, it tends to draw a few puzzled looks.

We don't care. Her family came from South Texas, and mine came from the South China Sea, but in terms of our personalities, we are two peas from the same pod. That's why our cultural differences have never been an issue in our relationship, although they have made for some entertaining times. The first time I met Becky's parents was following a game during the 1997 season. I'm quite certain I did more sweating during that post-game barbecue than I did during the entire game. I was so nervous about making a good impression that I could barely say a word. But her mom and dad, along with her brothers, went out of their way to make me feel at ease. I, on the other hand, probably went out of my way to make Becky feel a little uneasy when she met my family for the first time.

Following the 1997 season, we went to Rockport together to attend my brother's engagement party. In the Vietnamese culture, the engagement party is practically as big an event as the wedding. My entire family was coming into town, and my mother was staying up all night organizing the party and the massive amount of food that would be served. So, on our drive down to Rockport, I was kind of giving Becky a rundown of all the activities that would happen associated with the party. I also told her that if she happened to hear the words "di vay," she should simply go straight to the car and wait for me. She looked puzzled, and quickly asked me, "What does 'di vay' mean?" I told her it meant "go home" in Vietnamese, and if she heard that from my family members, it would mean that they didn't like her. I could barely keep from laughing as she sat in nervous silence for the rest of the trip. For the entire weekend, Becky smiled as much as possible and, during family discussions, looked as though she was watching a tennis match, with her head on a swivel, straining to hear the words, "di vay."

They were never uttered, and my family was almost as impressed with her as I was. They were impressed that she went to church with us on Sunday, where she was the only non-Asian in attendance. They were also impressed that she attempted to eat with chopsticks and that she seemed so genuinely interested in what everyone was saying despite the fact that she didn't understand a word of Vietnamese. She actually wasn't trying to comprehend anything; she was just listening for "di vay." But her interest made a good impression. The only uncomfortable moment of the weekend for Becky came after church when several of my family members asked me about her church denomination. We were all speaking in Vietnamese, and when I said she was Lutheran, the entire table shut up, turned, and stared at Becky. My dad then said the only English word he had uttered all day. "Lutheran?" he said in a somewhat disapproving tone. He and my other family members then began quizzing me about whether she would be willing to convert to Catholicism. As this discussion began, Becky really had her ears perked for "di vay."

I explained to my family that we had not yet discussed that possibility, and on the way back to College Station I explained to Becky why everyone seemed so concerned. To my family, Catholicism represented the reason we were here. My parents were raised in a Catholic church, and we were sponsored in this country by a Catholic church. I, too, am proud to be associated with the Catholic denomination, but it honestly doesn't mean the same to me as it does to my parents. While Becky and I were dating, we would take turns going to the Catholic church on one Sunday and the Lutheran church on the next. The Lutheran church was different for me in some ways, but in the most important way, it was the same. Jesus Christ was at the center of both churches, and I was resolute in only one regard—that we attended a church together where it was clear that the only way to salvation was through the blood of Jesus Christ. I explained to Becky that attending a church would be our joint decision, and I was open for discussion. She was also far more concerned about being a Christian than being a member of a certain denomination. After some discussions and prayers, we eventually settled on the Catholic church together, even though she had once told her mother that she would never change her denomination for a man.

It's funny how those "never" comments often change over time, as God reveals different plans for your life. Only a few years earlier, I had all but convinced myself that I would "never" amount to anything at Texas A&M. But as the 1997 season progressed, I found myself enjoying football and life as never before. My school work was going well, and I could see that I would earn my degree long before I completed my football eligibility. Spending time with Becky made my life away from the field much more enjoyable, and the season brought plenty of good times. We breezed through our first two games, whipping Sam Houston State 59–6 and gaining some serious retribution from the season before against Southwestern Louisiana. The cover of USL's 1997 media guide featured a picture of the scoreboard from our game the previous year when the Cajuns had upset us and registered the biggest win in the school's history. We made absolutely certain that they would need a different media guide cover the following year, building a 45–0 halftime lead en route to a 66–0 win.

It was pretty sweet redemption, but an even sweeter payback still awaited. We struggled in the first half against North Texas, but we closed with a flurry to beat the Eagles, 36–10. After three games, we were 3-0 and had gone from unranked in the preseason to No. 17 in the nation as we prepared for our first major test of the 1997 season at Colorado. This was a game that meant so much to us for so many reasons. First and foremost, it represented the first conference game of the season. But there were also other factors that added to the importance. Colorado ruined our season in 1995 and whipped us on our home field in '96 in the first Big 12 game for both teams. Furthermore, no one was really taking us seriously despite the fact that we were unbeaten. Some reporters were saying that we needed an asterisk by our record because we had not played anyone of note. That changed on October 4, 1997, when we faced No. 16 CU on its home turf.

In the first quarter, the Buffs jumped out to a 3–0 lead and had a golden opportunity to add to it later in the quarter. After we fumbled deep in our own territory, Colorado drove to our one-yard-line where the Buffs decided to go for it on fourth-and-goal. Now, one of the reasons I spend countless hours each week studying films is to look for tendencies that may come into play during the course of a game. It involves more than just looking at formations and how to defend particular plays. If you really study the intricacies of an opponent, you can often find little things that will clue you in to what play might be next. For example, a lineman might not get as far down in his stance if it's going to be a pass, or a receiver may cheat slightly toward the interior line if it's going to be a run. Noticing those little things can be the difference between making a big play or not. In Colorado's case, I had noticed on film that running back Herchell Troutman liked to line up a little bit farther back in the backfield when he was getting the ball on short yardage plays. He obviously wanted an extra few inches to get his speed going before he tried to leap over the top. Based on his stance and the overall formation on that fourth-and-goal, I guessed that Troutman was going to get the ball and would try to dive over the left side of the CU line of scrimmage. It turned out to be a good hunch.

When the ball was snapped, I knifed through the gap and met the blocking back head-on in the backfield. Rich Coady and I then wrapped up Troutman in the backfield for a three-yard loss. That proved to be a key moment in the game, and we scored the next 16 points to build a 16–3 lead by the fourth quarter. CU cut the lead to 16–10 early in the fourth quarter, and the Buffs had a chance to take the lead late in the game. But with three minutes left in the game and the Buffs on our twenty-eight yard line, Coady intercepted a John Hessler pass in the end zone to seal the win. It was the biggest regular-season win I had been part of since I arrived at A&M, and it was a testament to the value of hard work.

Three years earlier, Rich and I had been sitting around wondering aloud if we would ever play at Texas A&M. Instead of simply wondering, we created rivers of sweat, lifting longer and running more than any coach ever asked of us. I realize hard work doesn't always deliver the desired results. But in this particular case, our relentless efforts delivered results beyond our wildest expectations. Not only were we playing; we were making big plays in big games. We were having so much fun playing together and winning that Rich even began playing tricks on me during games. During a 56–17 win over Iowa State, I intercepted a pass for a touchdown early in the game, and we were in complete control late in the contest when Rich started messing with me in the huddle. Our players and coaches used to tease Rich all the time, saying that the sole reason he was actually playing was because he happened to be the only one who could interpret what I said in the huddle. Obviously, that wasn't true. Rich had proven to be a hell of a player, and I was working on being clearer in my enunciation. But with a big lead against the Cyclones, Rich began pulling pranks.

I always have my back to the opponents' offense in the huddle, so I can look toward the sideline for the defensive signals and then give the formation, the stunts, and the coverages to our defense. It is sometimes chaotic when the signal comes in late from the sideline and the offense breaks its huddle before I can call the defense. Well, against Iowa State, Rich started screaming at me, "Hurry up, Dat. They've already broken the huddle. They're at the line of scrimmage. Dat, call something, anything!" In a panic, I quickly called my own defense and then turned around to see Iowa State still in its huddle. I looked toward our sideline, and defensive coordinator Mike Hankwitz was looking at me as though I had lost my mind. He screamed something at me like, "What the heck are you doing?" When I turned back toward Rich, he was almost falling down he was laughing so hard. I gave him as stern a look as I could muster, but then I began laughing, too. It was just one example of the fun we were having through our first five games, as we were undefeated and climbing to No. 13 in the national polls.

The fun times came screeching to a halt the following week when Kansas State absolutely manhandled us in Manhattan. We managed only 90 yards of total offense the entire day, including minus-35 rushing yards, and the only thing that stayed on the field longer than our defense was the painted Wildcat emblem at midfield. We managed to stay relatively close for most of the day, holding K-State to three field goals in the first half, blocking a punt for a touchdown, and intercepting a pass that led to a touchdown. But we were thoroughly whipped. The final score was 35–17, but it really wasn't nearly that close. We were simply outmatched and overpowered by a better team. You can accept a loss like that much easier than you can stomach a loss like the one we had the following week at Texas Tech.

We were once again better than Tech, but for the third straight season, the Raiders managed to slip past us. We lost three fumbles, had some bad calls go against us, and couldn't stop Tech when it mattered most. With nineteen seconds left, they kicked the game-winning field goal, which hit off the left upright and bounced through to beat us 16–13. At 5-2 overall and 2-2 in the Big 12, we slipped to No. 25 in the polls and were in danger of slipping completely out of the Big 12 South race.

Most championship teams have a defining moment, and our moment came on November 1 at Kyle Field. We fell behind a good Oklahoma State team, 22–7, midway through the fourth quarter. We had not done much of anything offensively for the first 50 minutes of the game, but Branndon Stewart suddenly caught fire, delivering one clutch pass after another. We cut the lead to 22–14 with five minutes left, then tied it with 43 seconds left on a touchdown pass from Stewart to Chris Cole followed by a two-point conversion pass from Stewart to Sirr Parker. Then, in overtime, we held OSU to a field goal on its first possession and scored a touchdown on our first possession to win, 28–25.

That comeback victory generated a memorable celebration and propelled us to the Big 12 South Division title, as we whipped Baylor, Oklahoma, and a struggling Texas team to close the regular season. One year removed from the debacle of the 6-6 season in 1996, we were 9-2 and were the outright champions of the Big 12 South. It wasn't because we were any more talented in 1997. Quite honestly, we may have been even more talented in

'96. But our 1997 team had some qualities that the '96 team did not. We had genuine chemistry, and we developed a belief in each other. Unlike the 1996 team, we played much more for the name on the front of our jerseys than the names on the back. To a man, we were more focused on winning for Texas A&M than we were on impressing the NFL scouts. Even when we lost back-to-back games against Kansas State and Texas Tech and then fell 15 points behind Oklahoma State in the fourth quarter, we never lost our sense of purpose or our belief in each other.

It's been said many times that teams often take on the personality of their coaches. We may have had some of that going on in 1997, but I believe we really took on the personality of our leaders—Dan Campbell and Steve McKinney. We weren't flashy; we weren't heralded. But we carried a chip on our shoulder and refused to lose—just like Campbell and McKinney. I can't give those guys enough credit for instilling the belief throughout our '97 team that we would not repeat the struggles, the embarrassments, and the nosedives of 1996. We cratered in the face of adversity in 1996, but we rebounded from trying times in '97. There is so much parity in college and professional sports today that the difference between finishing first or fifth can many times be as simple as good chemistry. You can't time it, measure it, or weigh it, but you can definitely sense it.

To a certain extent, I believe you can also create it with the right people. Bill Parcells produced it during his first season with the Dallas Cowboys in 2003, establishing ground rules, practice habits, work ethic standards, disciplinary measures, and expectation levels from the moment he was first hired. We weren't that much more talented in 2003 than we had been in 2002. But Parcells immediately established a sense of belief in our locker room and then devised a meticulous method of operation that would deliver us from whipping boys to wildcard playoff representatives.

Parcells made it clear right from the start that the Cowboys were now his team. It was his way or the highway, and everyone on the roster was accountable to him. Perhaps, even subconsciously, we also became accountable to each other. We felt like we were all part of something unique, something unifying, something bigger than we had been part of in previous regimes. Almost overnight, we went from three straight seasons of 5-11 to 10-6 and were in the playoffs in 2003. Parcells didn't say any magical words or deliver any spine-tingling motivational speeches. He simply demanded more from all of us, established the consequences for failing to meet those demands, and transformed us from a bunch of paycheck collectors into a team. Because we had worked so much harder under Parcells, we also were far more reluctant to give in when adversity struck. Besides, Parcells himself worked so hard and was so thoroughly meticulous in every aspect of his preparations that most of us were more motivated by the desire not to let him down than we were by the fear of being cut or benched.

Parcells used basically the same formula for success in turning around the Cowboys that we had used in righting the Aggie ship. But instead of the coach being the primary source of accountability at A&M, it was Campbell and McKinney. We didn't want to let those guys down. Even some of the guys who may have been sitting on the fence when Campbell and McKinney initially made it clear that this was "their team" eventually wanted to make sure they were labeled as rope-holders and soldiers on their side of the fence. We developed strong bonds along the way, tasted some early success, and began to believe that we were part of something much bigger and better than we had experienced in 1996. I think it's no coincidence that one of the most meaningful personnel decisions the Cowboys made prior to the 2003 season was the addition of Dan Campbell. He caught only twenty passes for 195 yards during the 2003 season, but he once again was a unifying presence in the locker room. He was a natural leader and a tremendous chemistry addition to our team.

In 2004, when the Cowboys slipped back toward the bottom of the standings and failed to make the playoffs, we didn't have the same situation as the previous season. We had some significant injuries we had not endured the year before, including losing Campbell with a foot injury early in the season. Losing Dan for the entire season was a key reason why we slipped to 6-10 in 2004. You can't underestimate what he brought to our team in 2003. I've told Dan numerous times that he would make a heck of a coach if he ever decided to pursue that route. In fact, I've already pinned him with the "Little Tuna" nickname.

Back to Texas A&M, though—having said all that about what outstanding chemistry we developed in 1997, it didn't make much of a difference when we ran into a Big Red buzz saw on December 6 in San Antonio. Our reward for winning the South Division was a date with Nebraska for the Big 12 championship. All things considered, a date with a dentist's drill might have been more enjoyable. We were probably just happy to be in the title game after our bounce-back season, while the Cornhuskers were still steaming mad about losing the previous year's championship game to Texas. I don't know if I have ever played against a more focused, overpowering opponent than that Nebraska team. It was 16–0 at the end of the first quarter, and we were all feeling extremely fortunate about that because we had actually held the Huskers to three consecutive field goals. Then the floodgates opened in the second quarter, and the Huskers stormed to a 54–15 win en route to a share of the 1997 national championship.

Still, at 9-3 overall and as the champions of the Big 12 South, we earned an invitation to the Cotton Bowl to face another team on a mission: UCLA. Leading up to the game, the media made a big deal about how R. C. Slocum would be facing UCLA coach Bob Toledo, whom Slocum had fired as offensive coordinator following the 1993 season. The other story line involved how UCLA felt shafted for even being in the Cotton Bowl. The Bruins were ranked fifth nationally and had won nine straight games, including a 66–10 win over Houston and a 66–3 victory over Texas in Austin that effectively served as the beginning of the end for UT coach John Mackovic. UCLA believed it deserved to be in the Bowl Alliance, and it was so confident that it would whip us into oblivion that the Bruins came to Dallas with boxes of T-shirts that read "Texas State Champs."

Our focus was on finishing strong, earning some redemption from our lopsided loss to Nebraska, and representing one of our former stars, Reggie Brown. Ten days before we faced UCLA in the Cotton Bowl, Brown, who was then starting at linebacker for the Detroit Lions, had been temporarily paralyzed after slamming awkwardly into the back of a New York Jets lineman in a tackle that pushed Brown's head into his shoulders. Almost immediately, Brown's teammates realized he was not moving, and—worst of all—he wasn't breathing, either. Paramedics performed mouth-to-mouth resuscitation and later placed a breathing tube down Brown's throat, while players from both teams gathered in mini prayer sessions. As an ambulance escorted Brown out of the stadium, the steroid methylprednisolone was given to him in massive doses. Neurosurgeons later determined that Brown's injury was less severe than initially feared, and in a matter of days, he was walking again. At twenty-three years old, though, he was finished in the NFL.

When you play this game, you realize the physical risk you take. But when something like that happens to a friend like Reggie in the prime of a promising pro career, it hits home especially hard. At the NFL level, it reminds you not to take the paychecks for granted. Sooner or later, they will stop coming. If the average NFL player has been smart with his money, he will either have a fabulous financial head start on his post-football career or may never need to find a traditional, nine-to-five job. But far too many times, I see guys come into the NFL and immediately get caught in the extravagant lifestyle trap. There's a temptation to try to wear what Deion Sanders wears or drive what Michael Irvin drives or live in Emmitt Smith's neighborhood. But what most guys don't realize is that the contracts of a Sanders, Irvin, or Smith are the exception to the rule, not the norm. The average NFL career is roughly three seasons, and it can easily be cut shorter than that, as Reggie Brown can attest. When I heard the news about Reggie, I was distraught. I got to watch him closely in 1994 and to play with him in 1995, and he was the epitome of professionalism in how he handled himself on and off the field. So when Reggie got hurt, his injury was another reminder to me to play every game—every play, for that matter—as if it were going to be my last.

In Dallas at the Cotton Bowl we wanted to put Reggie's No. 59 on a patch on our helmets or jerseys, but a ridiculous NCAA rule prevented us from doing so. Instead, we wore his No. 59 on our undershirts and dedicated the game to his recovery. Despite being huge underdogs, we jumped all over UCLA in the first half, building a 16–0 lead. I intercepted a Cade McNown pass in the first quarter, returned it about twenty yards, and then pitched it back to defensive back Brandon Jennings, who took it the rest of the way for an eighty-three-yard touchdown that gave us a 7–0 lead. After the game, a reporter told me that he thought the lateral was a heads-up play, and I was almost tempted to tell him the truth. Almost. The truth of the matter is that I am pretty explosive covering short distances, and I receive plenty of comments and compliments about my first few steps. My eighty-third step, on the other hand, is nothing special, and I figured it would be much better to share the spotlight with Brandon Jennings than to run the risk of being caught from behind.

We still led 23–14 late in the third quarter, but UCLA rallied for a 29–23 win. I played one of my better games in an A&M uniform, recording twenty tackles, including a Cotton Bowl–record fifteen solo stops. Unfortunately, it wasn't enough. But even in the loss, we proved we were capable of standing toe-to-toe with one of the best teams in college football. We had opened the season with Sam Houston State and Southwestern Louisiana, but we closed it with consecutive games against Top 5 teams. We weren't good enough to win that kind of game yet, but we suddenly believed we were capable of taking the next step in 1998.

I also began to believe I was capable of taking the next step. I gave some thought to leaving school early and turning pro after the 1997 season, but I quickly realized I had some unfinished business to attend to at A&M. I had the opportunity to become the first graduate of an American university in my family. I was also on pace to become the all-time leading tackler in the history of Texas A&M. Individual honors are not usually a big motivational source for me, but the chance to become the number one tackler in the history of a university that has long prided itself on its defense—and particularly its linebackers—did have a nice appeal to me. I was also quite pleased with the way things were developing between Becky and me, and I was excited about seeing how our relationship would evolve. Finally, I figured that if we were able to go from middle-of-the-pack to champions of the South Division in one season, we might be capable of winning it all in 1998. I knew that I would kick myself for the rest of my life if I missed out on that opportunity. Besides, I knew that with McKinney gone, Campbell needed some help to lay the ground rules for the '98 season. I wasn't the outspoken leader or intimidating force that Campbell was, but I knew I could back him up and help him see to it that everyone was intent on eliminating distractions and focused on football. I thought I might even attempt to stretch beyond my comfort zone and provide some threats to anyone who missed practices or skipped out on weight room workouts. I couldn't intimidate them with a steely scowl like Dan, but I could probably scare the heck out of them by threatening to cut their "hair like Dat."

CHAPTER 10

The Lombardi and the "Oscar"

I'M NOT A SLAVE TO THEM, but I must reluctantly admit that I do have my superstitions. In fact, as a culture, the Vietnamese tend to be extremely susceptible to superstitions. Not just the well-known, garden variety, such as breaking mirrors, walking under a ladder, or allowing a black cat to cross your path. Many members of my own family, for example, won't allow a group picture to be taken unless there are an even number of people in the picture. You can take a photo of two, four, six, or eight of us, but don't even think about snapping a shot with only three, five, or seven of us. I realize that's a rather "odd" superstition, but aren't they all?

Another unusual Vietnamese superstition involves our homes. According to legend, you are not supposed to buy or build a home in which you can see the back door when you open the front door and enter the house. The reason for this is that, from a financial standpoint, "what flows in will flow right out." In other words, who needs financial planners as long as you have a nice dividing wall between the front door and the back? One particularly superstitious member of my family, my uncle Pho Do, has even taken over the unofficial title of "house supervisor" for all dwellings in our extended family. Pho will literally travel from his home in New Orleans to wherever a new house is being purchased or built and inspect it to make sure it meets the superstition standards. Even I realized this was absolutely absurd. So, when I found a nice, comfortable home in Flower Mound after signing my first contract with the Dallas Cowboys, I purchased it despite the fact that I could clearly see the back door when I walked in the front. But just to be on the safe side, I positioned a nice-sized plant in my home to obscure the view of the back door from the front entry. I figured that if there was at least the slightest truth to the legend, a few bucks would probably stick in the branches of the plant before heading out the back door.

As I said before, I'm not a slave to superstitions, but I am superstitious, especially when it comes to football. If something is working for me, I usually try to make sure I do it the same way every time. During my rookie season with the Cowboys, Becky gave me an impromptu little pep talk, a good luck message, as I walked out the front door. I played particularly well that game, so I have made certain that she gives me the exact same message before I walk out the door for every game. On one hurried occasion, I left the house with just a quick kiss from my wife and no message. As I began driving toward the stadium, I realized I was totally messing with the good luck vibes, so I circled back, came in the door, and told Becky I needed to leave all over again with the complete message. I could have played the game without it, but if I had blown out my knee in that game or missed the game-saving tackle, I would have never forgiven myself for not following the routine.

Once I arrive at the stadium, I am—like so many other players—meticulous with my pre-game rituals. During my rookie season, I often marveled at the painstaking process Deion Sanders followed for getting dressed for a game. Deion would lay out his complete uniform—shoes, socks, pants, jersey, sweat bands, and everything else—on the floor in front of his locker before he ever thought of putting any of it on. He laid it out in the form of a person, almost as though he was creating a Deion shrine before the actual Deion dressed. But no one ever questioned it. It obviously worked for Deion, and if it works, the rule of thumb in the athletic world is to keep doing it.

My pre-game ritual isn't as elaborate as some, but I make sure to do everything the "right" way before the left. I pull my right pants leg on first, put my right glove on first, have my right ankle taped first, slip my right arm through my shoulder pads first, and so forth. I know I could put my left leg in my pants first, but if I were to do so and then miss a tackle, I would—during the middle of a game—suddenly be overcome by a nagging, haunting thought that I had messed with the pre-game karma and paid the price. I can only imagine being interviewed after such a series of events:

Reporter: What were you thinking after you missed that tackle, Dat?

Me: I was kicking myself for not putting my right leg in my pants first.

I know it sounds ridiculous, but that's certainly no more absurd than what became our good luck charm during the Aggies' Big 12 championship season of 1998. I am almost too embarrassed even to acknowledge this, but one of my facial hairs took on a life of its own in '98, serving as one of the most bizarre mascots you could possibly imagine.

But first, a little background: Following the end of the spring academic semester in 1998, virtually everyone on the roster

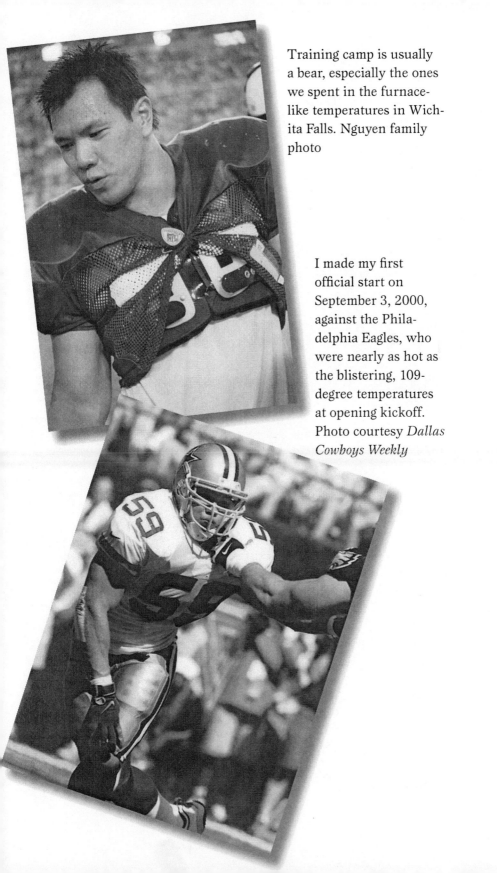

Training camp is usually a bear, especially the ones we spent in the furnace-like temperatures in Wichita Falls. Nguyen family photo

I made my first official start on September 3, 2000, against the Philadelphia Eagles, who were nearly as hot as the blistering, 109-degree temperatures at opening kickoff. Photo courtesy *Dallas Cowboys Weekly*

I obviously never had the chance to play for the legendary Tom Landry, but I considered it an honor to wear his commemorative hat decal on our jerseys the year he died. Photo courtesy *Dallas Cowboys Weekly*

You literally have to be on your toes every play in the NFL. Photo courtesy *Dallas Cowboys Weekly*

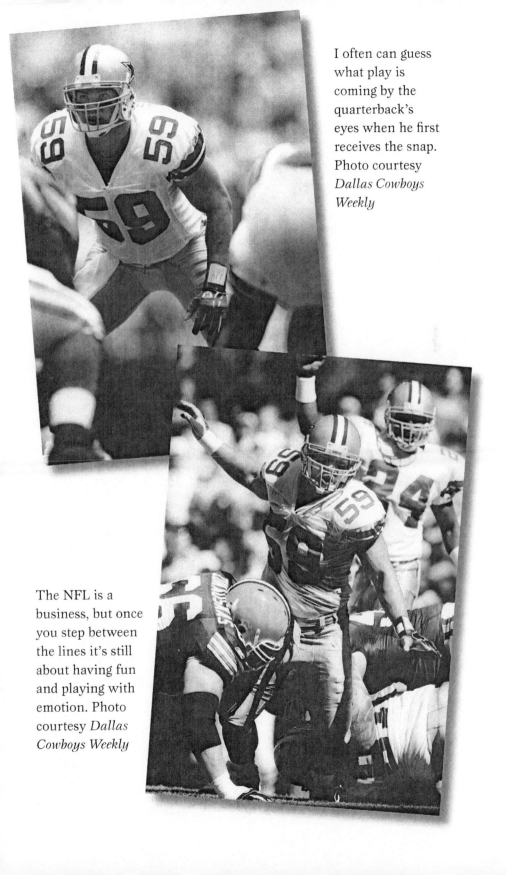

I often can guess what play is coming by the quarterback's eyes when he first receives the snap. Photo courtesy *Dallas Cowboys Weekly*

The NFL is a business, but once you step between the lines it's still about having fun and playing with emotion. Photo courtesy *Dallas Cowboys Weekly*

I was beginning to develop a reputation of having stone hands until I intercepted three passes in 2004. Photo courtesy *Dallas Cowboys Weekly*

Sometimes referees need help. I just wanted to remind them here that it's our ball. Photo courtesy *Dallas Cowboys Weekly*

At our rehearsal, I kept thinking how lucky
I was to have two such special women in my life
—Becky and my mom. Nguyen family photo

The first time I met Becky's parents,
Kenneth and Myrna Foster, was following an A&M
football game. I was sweating more at that meeting than during the game.
But they are incredible in-laws and did an incredible job raising their kids.
Nguyen family photo

Long before Becky delivered our first child, I knew she would be a great mother. My niece seems to agree, as she and Becky prepare to go to our wedding. Nguyen family photo

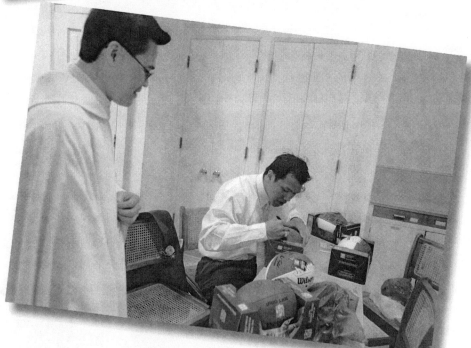

I'm sometimes amazed at the timing of autograph requests. Here, I sign a few footballs before our wedding. Nguyen family photo

I thank God for so much in my life, especially my wonderful wife. Nguyen family photo

March 10, 2001, is one of the happiest days of my life. I'm just thrilled she said, "I do." Nguyen family photo

Sam, Coach Phil, and Maddie Bennett share the excitement of our wedding day. I believe Nancy was all smiles as she looked down on us. Nguyen family photo

Our 2004 Christmas Card picture. The best present I received was knowing that Becky was pregnant at the time with our second child. Nguyen family photo

The original "Bad Company"—Becky, Aubrey and Dat. Hopefully, we will need to do a second printing of this book to include pictures of "Datty's" second little angel, who was born in July of 2005. Nguyen family photo went home for a brief stint. Dan Campbell, Rich Coady, and I stuck around, though, to continue to work out in preparations for our final season. The three of us talked daily about what it would take to get us over the hump and win it all. The way we played against UCLA in the Cotton Bowl had given us an indication of just how close we were to being one of the elite teams in college football. So we decided, then and there, that we would have each other's back. If Dan said something to the team, Rich and I would back him up. If Rich said something, Dan and I would support him. And if I said something to the team, Rich would first interpret it and then Dan would back it up.

As the rest of the team came back for summer workouts in late May and early June, Dan came up with the idea of weekly team get-togethers. The chemistry had been good in '97, but he wanted to do something to make it even better in '98. Dan's suggestion: keg parties. You won't find this anywhere in Vince Lombardi's "What it takes to be No. 1" speech or in any other self-help book on building champions. But Dan's logic was that the team that parties together will eventually celebrate together, and the team that works hard together should relax together. Honestly, I initially thought it was a little outlandish, but hey, we had made a vow to have each other's back, so I decided to lend the plan my support. All week, we'd work like plow horses, pumping iron in the weight room and frying in the scorching heat and humidity while running on the artificial turf practice fields. Then, each weekend, we would gather, usually at Dan's place, to share a few beers and bond together as a team. While attendance was not mandatory at these get-togethers, it was definitely frowned upon if someone failed to show. Considering that the harshest frown came from Dan, everybody usually showed up.

A football team can become an extremely divided, segregated group. You often have your black players here and your white players there. You also have the divisions of upper classmen and newcomers, and there can be a big separation between the offense and the defense. I have to give Dan a ton of credit here. Those beer and barbecue get-togethers united us as a team as we had never been before. It didn't matter if you were white or black, Asian or All-American, starter or walk-on. When we came together that summer, we lost our cliques and found ourselves as a team. And when we went to New York to open the season on national television against No. 2–ranked Florida State, we truly believed we were capable of beating the Seminoles. We were huge underdogs for the Kickoff Classic, but after our last two games of '97, we were accustomed to that role. At halftime, when we went to the locker room with a 14–10 lead, the members of our team may have been the only people in America who weren't stunned.

Unfortunately, Florida State blanked us in the second half, and the Seminoles escaped with a 23–14 win. We earned some national respect that night for the way we battled, but I vividly recall the feeling of frustration in our locker room. We had not come to New York for a moral victory or to make it respectable; we had come to win. We failed to do that, but I could tell by the resolute looks on our players' faces that we were growing as a team. Speaking of "growing" and "faces," I first noticed the little, black whisker sprouting from my right cheek shortly after our loss to FSU. When I first noticed it, I thought to myself, "I'll shave that off when I get the chance." But unlike Dan "Grizzly Adams" Campbell, I don't need to shave every day. In fact, I probably couldn't grow a full beard if I spent the rest of my life on a deserted island. So, I just never got around to shaving it as we prepared for our first home game of the season against an extremely explosive Louisiana Tech team. We shut down the Bulldogs and then followed up that win with victories over Southern Mississippi, North Texas, and Kansas.

We were now 4-1, and—here's the superstitious side of me—

when I looked at that growing whisker in the mirror, I began thinking, "We haven't lost since that whisker showed up. It's staying." It was also continuing to grow. It had even begun to curl a little, and when Campbell and Coady began noticing it and poking fun at me for it, I explained the logic for keeping it. They, of course, thought it was absurd, but as athletes, they also understood the "if it's working, don't mess with it" theory. So, they named the whisker Oscar, and it became a running joke and growing good luck charm.

We needed all the luck we could muster as we prepared for our sixth game of the season against Nebraska. The defending national champions had pasted a 54–15 whipping on us at the end of the previous season, but this time, they had to come to Kyle Field. And this time, we knew things would be different. The Huskers still possessed plenty of firepower, but after watching the tapes of their games from earlier in the season, we knew they were not the same team that had manhandled us the year before. They were ranked No. 2 in the polls and they had won forty straight regular-season conference games. But they were also vulnerable in certain areas. We watched the tape of their game the week before and noticed that Oklahoma State was actually controlling the line of scrimmage. Nebraska managed to win the game, but OSU had exposed some weaknesses. During the week leading up to our game against Nebraska, our intensity and our confidence continued to grow as we realized that this was a very winnable game.

On the morning of October 10, we could all sense a magic in the air. The weather was perfect, and our crowd was incredible. Virtually every fan in the stadium that day wore a maroon T-shirt as part of the first-ever Maroon Out, and when I looked up in the stands prior to the game it looked like an ant bed that had been stirred and was now in attack mode. I don't think I've ever been so excited for a game in my life.

On the second play of the game, I reached to make a tackle, as a swarm of my teammates converged on the Nebraska ball carrier. As I was getting up, my right thumb suddenly began throbbing in pain. I have a pretty high pain tolerance, and I can usually shake things off quickly. I even remember, as a four- or five-year-old kid, helping my dad out along the docks of Rockport and trying to push the shrimp boat away from the dock. I wasn't strong enough at the time, and the boat banged against the wooden pier, smashing my right thumb. That hurt, but nothing like it hurt in the Nebraska game. As I was walking back to the huddle, the throbbing went from bothersome to brutal. On the game's second play, as I was trying to wrap up the ball carrier, my teammate, Roylin Bradley came flying in from the outside and smashed my right thumb between his helmet and the ball carrier's. As I looked down at my right hand and tried to shake it off, I noticed that my thick Nike glove was filling with blood that was dripping onto my pants and pouring onto the field. Rich Coady looked at my bloody mitt and said, "Dat, get the hell outta here and get that fixed."

But it was third down, and I figured that if we could stop Nebraska on third down, I could get to the sideline and get my thumb looked at without ever missing a play. Fortunately, that's what happened. If the Huskers had converted on third down, I might have passed out on the next series. Instead, I got to the sideline and one of our trainers cut the glove off and saw that my thumb was broken and cut to the bone. We ran under the tunnel on the west side of Kyle Field, and the trainers began stitching me up. Then they put a huge pad around my thumb and taped it back up. Just as they were taping it, I heard our crowd go nuts. Our quarterback, Randy McCown, had just hit Chris Taylor on an eighty-one-yard touchdown pass. I told our trainers to hurry it up because there was no way I wanted to miss any of this game. For the next three and one-half quarters, our guys stepped up and played like champions. Dante Hall, Ja'Mar Toombs, War-rick Holdman, Ron Edwards, McCown, Taylor, and so many others came up with big plays at the most opportune moments as we built a 28–7 lead in the fourth quarter. Even when Ne-braska came back to cut it to 28–21, another unsung hero, Sedric Curry, stepped up with the game-saving interception to preserve A&M's first victory over a Top 5 team since 1975. The team that had partied together in the summer now had a legitimate reason to celebrate together.

We did, on Saturday night, but we also knew we had to keep things in perspective. We returned to work on Sunday and then continued to grind out wins. We beat Baylor the following week and then finally beat Texas Tech the next week. After that, we beat Oklahoma State in a game in which I became the leading tackler in A&M history. That was a nice individual honor, but we were all caught up in more meaningful team goals. In early November, we blanked Oklahoma, 29–0, and then wrapped up our second consecutive Big 12 South title by beating a tough, ex-tremely physical Missouri team, 17–14, at Kyle Field. In a span of two and a half months, we had rolled off ten straight victories and had climbed to No. 6 in the national polls. All that stood between us and a perfect record in Big 12 play was the annual grudge match with Texas.

Now, I'm not suggesting that this actually has anything to do with the reason we lost to Texas, but it was a bad omen in my superstition book when just days before our game against the Longhorns, Oscar inexplicably fell off my face. I just woke up one morning, and Oscar was gone. Once the game began, Ricky Williams was also "gone," more times than I care to remember. Williams came into the game with a good chance of breaking Tony Dorsett's all-time NCAA rushing record. Instead, he shat-tered it, rushing for 259 yards as the Longhorns built a 23–7 lead over us in the fourth quarter. We didn't play well on either side of the ball for the first 51 minutes of the game, but as was typical of our 1998 team, we never gave up. We rallied to take a 24–23 lead when McCown clawed his way into the end zone on a fourth-down option play with 2:20 left in the game. But instead of turning up the heat on redshirt freshman quarterback Major Applewhite, we went into a prevent defense, allowing Applewhite to pick us apart. In the end, our prevent defense only prevented us from winning, as UT kicked a field goal with five seconds left, to beat us 26–24. Our ten-game winning streak was over, and we slipped all the way to No. 10 in the polls.

To make matters worse, we lost McCown, who in terms of leadership and fiery attitude could have been considered our offensive mini-Dan, for the Big 12 championship game. McCown had separated his shoulder while fighting his way into the end zone for the go-ahead touchdown against Texas, leaving the quarterback duties to the once-forgotten Branndon Stewart. Our opponent in the Big 12 title game was once again the nation's best team. A year earlier, we had faced a Nebraska team that was practically a machine for the Big 12 title. Watching tape of the 1998 Kansas State Wildcats brought back some eerily familiar memories. K-State had whipped us in 1997, and the Wildcats were much better in '98. They came to Saint Louis with a dominant defense, an explosive offense, a spectacular kicking game, and a seventeen-game winning streak. The Wildcats were ranked No. 1 in one of the national polls and needed to beat us and have Miami beat UCLA to have a chance to play for the national championship in the Tostitos Fiesta Bowl.

K-State looked as if it was well on its way to playing for the national championship—and probably winning it—in the third quarter when the Wildcats went up 27–15 and the announcement was made that Miami had, indeed, beaten UCLA. The crowd at the Trans World Dome, which was filled mostly with purple-clad K-State fans, went nuts. Even the Wildcats' players burst into mini-celebrations on the field. I heard several of them shout, "We're going to the Fiesta Bowl, we're going to play for the national title." But in the words of ESPN's Lee Corso, we basically said, "Not so fast, my friends." There was still a quarter to play, and we had been down this road before. Stewart had led us to an overtime victory over Oklahoma State the year before after being fifteen points behind, and we had rallied from a sixteen-point deficit the week before against Texas. We weren't about to quit, and Kansas State suddenly realized it had everything to lose.

Stewart caught fire early in the fourth quarter, and he hit Leroy Hodge for a touchdown pass that cut the lead to 27–19. After we began shutting down the K-State offense, our offense once again drove deep into K-State territory before the Wildcats stopped us on a big fourth-down play. All K-State really needed was one first down to wrap up the game, but Warrick Holdman stripped quarterback Michael Bishop of the ball after Bishop had gained the necessary yardage for a first down, and Cornelius Anthony recovered it. Given another chance, Stewart made the Wildcats pay. He hit Matt Bumgardner, who made an incredible catch, and later connected with Sirr Parker on a nine-yard touchdown pass with just over a minute left in the game. He then hit Parker again on a two-point conversion pass that tied it up at 27–27. Once we got it tied, we just knew there was no way we were going to let it slip away. We traded field goals in the first overtime and then held K-State to another field goal in the second overtime. That's when Stewart caught lightning in a bottle once again, as we faced third-and-seventeen at the K-State thirty-two. Stewart hit Parker again on a quick slant, and Parker hit the front pylon for a touchdown that gave us an amazing 36–33 win in double overtime.

As we piled on top of each other and celebrated one of the most improbable victories I've ever seen—let alone been a part of—we crumpled many of the huge tortilla chips that K-State fans had been throwing onto the field earlier in the game. Kansas State's players were so stunned that many of them couldn't even shake our hands. Many of their fans also stayed in their seats for some time, sitting in shocked disbelief at what had just happened. Honestly, I can sympathize with K-State's dazed demeanor. To this day, it's still rather amazing to me that we won that game. So many things had to happen for us to win, and so many of our players had to come up with big plays. It would probably be easier to list the guys who didn't come up with a difference-making play than to attempt to name all the ones who did.

Kansas State was undoubtedly the more talented team. If we had played the Wildcats ten times that season, they might have beaten us in eight or nine of those games. But winning that one game and holding up the Big 12 championship trophy in the locker room afterward reinforced a belief that had been implanted deep within my mind by my parents many years earlier: Those who are willing to fight through any setback are better prepared to make any comeback. We were the comeback kids in 1998, rallying from a deficit in five of our eleven wins.

We almost did it again in the Sugar Bowl against an Ohio State team that may have been the best team we played all year. The Buckeyes scored 21 points in a span of 6 minutes and 35 seconds in the first quarter to take a 24–7 lead into the locker room at the half. But we battled back and had a golden opportunity to cut the lead to three in the third quarter. Unfortunately, the Buckeyes came up with the key plays and held on for a 24–14 win.

The loss to Ohio State in the Sugar Bowl did not diminish what we had accomplished in 1998. We had traveled from the Big Apple to the Big Easy, faced four Top 5–ranked teams, stunned Nebraska, shocked Kansas State, claimed A&M's first Big 12 championship, and put the Aggies back on the map of the nation's elite teams. We worked our tails off and created some of our own breaks. We were lucky at times and just plain good at others. But our simplest recipe for success was belief. We believed so strongly in each other and in our dreams that we refused to believe we were ever out of a game. The power of a person's belief cannot be measured, but it can also not be underestimated.

My belief in myself would again be tested in the months after our remarkable run to the Big 12 title. Following our win over Kansas State, I was invited to a black-tie affair at the Hyatt Regency in Houston for the presentation of the 1998 Lombardi Award. The award, named in honor of legendary coach Vince Lombardi, is presented annually to the nation's top interior lineman on either side of the ball and is chosen by a panel of more than three hundred media members, college coaches, and past winners. It's an extremely prestigious award, and I was in contention because I had assembled some pretty good career numbers, starting fifty-one consecutive games and recording 517 tackles—62 more than the previous A&M record holder, two-time All-American Johnny Holland. Even with those numbers, I went to Houston on December 8 believing I would be little more than a dressed-up observer. After all, the other three finalists were Wisconsin offensive tackle Aaron Gibson, Ohio State linebacker Andy Katzenmoyer, and Georgia offensive tackle Matt Stinchcomb. Katzenmoyer probably had the biggest name of the bunch, and Ohio State had produced more Lombardi Award winners (five) than any other school. So, I was pleasantly surprised when the presenter of the award, former Dallas Cowboys quarterback Roger Staubach, stepped to the microphone and announced, "Gig 'em, Aggies," in honor of my being selected as the winner.

I was just as pleased and surprised a short time later when I was named the winner of the 1998 Chuck Bednarik Award, which is given each year to the nation's top defensive player.

With those awards, along with unanimous All-American and All-Big 12 recognition, I was feeling pretty good about myself and my future. I went out and bought a new car because I figured that if I was good enough to earn those kinds of awards and that type of recognition, I was also good enough to be one of the first few linebackers selected in the 1999 NFL Draft. I figured wrong.

The New Orleans Saints had shown a considerable amount of pre-draft interest in me, and leading up to the draft I had actually spent some face-to-face time interviewing with Rick Venturi, who was, at the time, the linebackers coach for the Saints. We hit it off well, and the Saints seemed genuinely interested in me, even suggesting that I would be selected by them in the second round. That sounded like a pretty good scenario for me since I still had family in New Orleans, and I had just played my final game at A&M in New Orleans. I also liked the idea of staying in the South, and I knew several of their players, including former A&M linebacker Keith Mitchell. I was so excited the night before the draft, thinking about the possibilities of winding up with the Saints and other potential scenarios, that I barely slept a wink.

I was anxious to find out where my future home would be, but one thing I didn't want to do was sit in front of the television all day and wait. Instead, I took Becky to Rockport on the Friday night before the first day of the draft and arranged to help a friend move. After we helped him get settled, we went to a birthday party for another friend, just as the draft began. We finally wound up back at my parents' house around mid-afternoon because my mother had invited a bunch of friends and family over to help me celebrate. I assumed we would be all done by about 3:00 or 4:00 in the afternoon, but by the time everyone began arriving at my parents' house, there was still no reason to celebrate. My initial thought about landing in New Orleans went up in smoke early in the first round when the Saints traded all of their draft picks to select Ricky Williams with the No. 5 overall pick. All of my fellow finalists for the Lombardi Award—Stinchcomb, Katzenmoyer, and Gibson—also went in the first round, along with fellow linebackers Chris Claiborne and Al Wilson.

When the first round finally came to an end, I was a little disappointed, but not surprised. I knew NFL teams would look more at my height than at my heart and would base their firstround decisions more on body dimensions than tackle totals. The knock on me coming into the draft was that I was too small to play middle linebacker in the NFL. But I took some comfort in the fact that Mike Singletary, whom I had been compared to by several coaches and scouts, was passed up in the first round nearly two decades earlier because of the same physical limitations. So, Becky and I finally settled onto the couch and hoped I would receive the call in the second round. It didn't come.

Linebackers Barry Gardner, Mike Peterson, Rahim Abdullah, and Johnny Rutledge all went within the first twenty picks of the second round, but my phone still wasn't ringing. I was getting a little antsy, and so were my house guests. My mother didn't want to serve any food until there was a cause for celebration. As the third round progressed, Rex Tucker went to the Bears with the fifth pick and then Rich Coady went to the Saint Louis Rams with the seventh pick. I was thrilled for them, but I was growing more and more anxious, thinking to myself, "Did I do something wrong at the NFL Combine?"

The NFL Combine is an annual event in Indianapolis where the top college prospects are timed, tested, weighed, and measured in every conceivable way by NFL scouts and coaches. It usually plays an important role in the draft status of players, and I thought I did well. As the third round continued, I began to question that assumption.

At about the midway point of the third round, I fully expected the Kansas City Chiefs to take me with the fourteenth pick. I knew they needed a linebacker, and, sure enough, they took one. Just not me. The Chiefs took Gary Stills from West Virginia, and four picks later, the New York Giants took Dan Campbell. Then, when Tampa Bay took Kansas State place kicker Martin Gramatica with the next pick, I really began to worry—not only about my own draft status but also about the temperament of all the hungry people inside my parents' home. After the Buccaneers took a kicker over me, I turned to Becky and said, "Honey, I think I may have bought that new car a little too soon."

Finally, at about 8:15—some five hours after I had thought I would be selected—my phone rang. It was Jerry Jones, the owner of the Dallas Cowboys, and Dave Campo, the defensive coordinator. They informed me that they were going to select me with the twenty-fourth pick of the third round and the eighty-fifth pick overall. To be honest, I was initially more relieved that the wait was over than I was overjoyed at the realization I had been drafted. Once I broke the news to everyone in my parents' home, a big celebration began—primarily because it was finally time to eat.

It was one of the longest, most stressful days of my life, but the extended wait was probably a blessing in disguise. I knew people doubted whether I would be able to play in the NFL because of my size, and watching all those linebackers go in the draft in front of me made me hungrier to prove that I could play at the next level. Jerry Jones told me on the phone that he really didn't think I would still be available with the eighty-fifth pick, and he made me feel good about becoming a part of the Cowboys' organization. Dave Campo then told me that he loved the way I played the game and said he was looking forward to coaching me. I told them before I hung up the phone that they would not be sorry for drafting me, that I would not let them down.

Following the draft, I flew to Dallas for a press conference where all of the Cowboys' draft picks were introduced. In addition to picking me in the third round, the Cowboys also selected Ebenezer Ekuban, Solomon Page, Wane McGarity, Hunndens "Peppi" Zellner, Martay Jenkins, Mike Lucky, and Kelvin Garmon. Interestingly, when I reported to the 2004 training camp in Oxnard, California, I was the only member of the 1999 draft class still on the team. That just goes to show how quickly things can change in the NFL and how fleeting a pro football career can be. You cannot take anything for granted in the NFL. If you do, you will quickly be granted a one-way ticket home.

After the press conference, I went home to Rockport and then back to College Station to relax a little and work out a lot. On the one hand, I felt as though I had, indeed, made it to the big time. Against some of the longest odds, I had made it to the NFL. The little Vietnamese kid whom almost no one wanted on their youth soccer team was now part of "America's Team." It was an incredibly satisfying realization. I thanked God, I thanked my parents, I thanked my junior high, high school, and college coaches. I felt blessed beyond my wildest dreams, and after the initial disappointment of being selected late in the third round, I also felt incredibly lucky to have been selected by the Cowboys. I would be able to stay in Texas, where my family, friends, and all the Aggie fans who had followed me in college would be able to continue watching me. Ebenezer Ekuban and I became fast friends, and we wound up living together in an extended-stay motel for a short time prior to going to training camp. He always used to joke about how he was the only first-round draft pick in the league who was continually in the shadows of the third-round draft pick. When we would go out in public together, whether we were at the grocery store or a restaurant, people would often recognize me and not him. I assured him it would be the other way around if we were playing for the Carolina Panthers, just down the road from where he played his college ball at North Carolina. He didn't buy it. He was always saying stuff like, "I know you had a bunch of tackles in college, but all these Aggies treat you like you're some kind of movie star." I simply reminded Ebenezer that he was no longer in North Carolina. He was in Texas, where many people remember the Alamo, but they never, ever forget their football heroes. Ebenezer finally got the picture when I told him to think about how passionate North Carolina fans were about basketball. Then I told him to double that and he would have a good idea about the passionate nature of A&M football fans.

As that reality began to sink in with Ebenezer, the reality of being part of one of the most storied franchises in all of professional sports began to sink in with me. It thrilled me, but when I reported to my first training camp in Wichita Falls, Texas, it also was more than a bit nerve-racking. First of all, I had known it was going to be hot, but I had never thought I would actually be able to touch the sun. I remember being relieved when the temperature dipped into the low 100s.

Of course, the real source of nervous perspiration wasn't the sun; it was the stars. I looked around the field that first day and saw Troy Aikman, Michael Irvin, Emmitt Smith, Deion Sanders, and Larry Allen—all guys who are destined for the Hall of Fame. I'm not easily star-struck, but those guys had been the nucleus of the great Cowboys teams of the mid-1990s, a group that won three Super Bowls in a span of four years and dominated the NFL like few franchises have ever come close to doing. I was still a goofy high school kid in Rockport when Aikman, Irvin, and Smith were just beginning their assaults on the NFL record books. Quite frankly, as I looked out on the field and watched these superstars at work, I was kind of wondering if I was supposed to tackle those guys or ask them for their autographs.

When we weren't on the field or in meetings, I remember staring into the mirror quite a bit during that first training camp.

Part of the time, I was reminding myself I could do it, telling myself that I could handle it, and convincing myself that I belonged here. The other part of the time, I was looking—and hoping—for any signs of another Oscar reappearance on my face. I didn't know what the future had in store for me, but I knew I could use all the good luck and good omens I could find.

CHAPTER 11

Moving and (Milk)shaking

I THINK IT'S PROBABLY ABOUT TIME I came clean on some things regarding my lifestyle. Many of the sports books you see on shelves today feature some scandalous revelation about a professional athlete's lifestyle, so I feel compelled to do the same, shedding some light on my own secret life away from the glamour of the gridiron. Here it is in a nutshell: I'm really a rather simple homebody, who would much rather spend an evening painting the living room with my wife than painting the town red. I love being at home, love hanging out with my daughter, and prefer to be in the "lamp" light of my living room than in the neon glow of a club scene. And the last time I stayed up all night it was a result of colic, not Coors.

There you have it. The secret is out. I live what some of my teammates might consider a pretty dull existence, and I cherish every minute of it. I certainly don't condemn anybody for bar-hopping, partying, or enjoying the nightlife scene. I did some of that in college, and I still don't mind joining the boys for a couple of beers every once in a while. But what really makes me happy and what I look forward to most is simply being at home with my family. Aside from my old friend Oscar, I don't have many wild hairs.

Besides, I am also more frugal than flamboyant. Once in a blue moon, Becky and I enjoy going out to a romantic restaurant. Nine times out of ten, however, we would prefer to sip on a McDonald's milkshake instead of a bottle of merlot. I catch myself looking at the price of a bottle of wine at a four-star restaurant and thinking about how many days my father would have had to work on his shrimp boat to pay for that single bottle. Remember, I come from an upbringing in which my father and a friend would, from time to time, share a single beer after a particularly long day. Coming from that background, I don't necessarily mind spending money, but I detest the thought of wasting it. Partly because of all that my mother and father overcame, I am absolutely committed to avoiding anything that would ever disgrace my family name.

That's why I take a tremendous amount of pride in trying to keep my name out of the majority of newspaper headlines. I enjoy receiving compliments and praise from the media as much as the next guy, but I don't crave the spotlight, and I don't need to see my name in bold print. Becky and I don't even subscribe to the newspapers. Some guys say they don't pay attention to what the newspapers say about them; I don't even have it delivered. Becky always jokes that I have probably had more articles written about me than the total number of newspaper stories I have ever read—on any subject. I sincerely wish I had more of a desire to read, but quite frankly, I usually read only the Bible for my own benefit or Dr. Seuss for my kids' entertainment. Family members and friends sometimes call and let me know if an article has been written about me, and an associate of mine puts those articles on a web site. But I will only occasionally take the time to read them. I have noticed over the years that fewer and fewer reporters even bother to interview me. It's not that the media has anything against me. The reporters have just finally figured out that—compared with some of the other extravagant personalities that reside in a typical NFL locker room—I am pretty darned dull.

When I entered the NFL in 1999, a number of regional and national publications did stories on me primarily because of my family background and Asian heritage. There was even a nice story about me in *Esquire* magazine, titled "A Vietnamese Cowboy?" A scantily clad Charlize Theron was on the cover of the magazine, which probably created quite a debate among the publication's editors. One can only imagine how long it must have taken them to choose Charlize in spaghetti straps over me in shoulder pads for the cover shot.

Although I'll never win a cover battle with Charlize or any other sex symbol, I am convinced that I could be a more high-profile player in terms of media exposure if I sought it a little more. In this league, you see it all the time. The guys who taunt and dance on the field inevitably wind up in front of the cameras after the game. If you say outlandish things about opponents, teammates, coaches, or fans, you are practically guaranteed to be a media darling. Guys know how to play the media to draw attention to themselves, and the added publicity often leads to more Pro Bowl votes, more commercial endorsements, and more money in their pockets. But I prefer not to purposely draw attention to myself because of any antics on the field, and I see no reason to say controversial things about anyone in the post-game setting.

First of all, that kind of nonsense makes you a target. This league is rough enough without placing a bulls-eye on your chest. But more important to me, I think self-promotion and trash-talking tend to make guys look foolish. Impromptu celebrations with your teammates following a big play are part of the game and add excitement to the moment. But the individual, choreographed, and prearranged celebrations are, in my opinion, self-serving and detract from the team concept.

What seems ironic to me is that many of the guys who try to stand out from their teammates because of their outrageousness are often the same guys who claim they hate the glare of the public spotlight and have no responsibility to the fans. From the time I first began receiving autograph requests and making public appearances at Texas A&M, I have taken very seriously my "role model" responsibility. I remember years ago when Charles Barkley made a big deal out of not being a role model just because he was a professional athlete. He said some things that made sense, noting that parents should be the primary role models for kids. In a perfect world, I would agree wholeheartedly with Barkley's comments. I, for one, am extremely lucky to have two incredible, hard-working parents who are undoubtedly my role models. But I also realize that in today's society, not everyone is so fortunate. In my work with various charitable organizations, I frequently come in contact with kids from broken homes who are looking *for* one or both of their parents—not looking up to them. I've played with many guys from that kind of background, and I've seen many kids who battle through extremely difficult home situations.

Like it or not, those kids are often looking to the professional sports world for role models. When you're in the NFL, NBA, or any other professional league, you're a public figure in a prime-time spotlight. Kids want your autograph; they want to wear your jersey; they want to move like you and imitate you. I'm certainly not a superstar compared with many of the most prominent players in the NFL. But when I slip on that jersey and step onto that field I realize I have thousands of young, impressionable eyes on me. Plenty of pro athletes love the endorsements and contracts that come because of the high-profile nature of the game, but some don't like the responsibility that comes with the territory. Some refuse to accept it; I choose to embrace it. That's one of the primary reasons I do not have any body piercings or tattoos, for instance, although I have absolutely nothing against guys who fill their arms with ink and ears with gold. I'm not going to give my own kids—or anyone else's kids who are watching me—justification for tattooing or piercing their own bodies just because I have. Nor am I going to taunt, trash-talk, push an official, punch a coach, or anything else that would make me the embarrassing lead item on SportsCenter. It's not my style, and I don't ever want to embarrass my family, my friends, or the fans who indirectly pay my salary.

Now, I obviously wouldn't mind making the lead highlight reel on SportsCenter because of something I had done positively on the field, but I would want to do it in a classy, dignified, and understated manner—much like two of my early role models on the Cowboys. I developed some quick friendships with some of the younger players on the Cowboys as soon as we began the 1999 training camp in Wichita Falls. I will likely always be friends with all-around good guys like Ebenezer Ekuban, Dexter Coakley, and several other players I met in the early days with the Cowboys. But among the big-name stars who were still on the roster when I arrived in 1999, I was particularly impressed with the way Troy Aikman and Darren Woodson handled themselves. "Woody" was a seven-year veteran when I came into the league, and he was a five-time member of the Pro Bowl team. He retired at the end of the 2004 season as the leading tackler in the history of the Cowboys, and he is destined for the Hall of Fame. Inside the locker room, though, he was just a normal, good-natured, level-headed guy. Woodson did his talking by the way he played on Sundays, and he kept his mug shot in the media guide and out of the police blotter. The same goes for Aikman, who entered the league in 1989 and left it in 2000 as one of the NFL's all-time best quarterbacks. Aikman had superstar credentials, but he also possessed the humility of a country boy who never forgot his roots were in boots. He was the consummate professional and the poised leader of a proud franchise. He had money, fame, three Super Bowl rings, and every reason to be arrogant. But that was simply not Aikman's personality. He never acted as though he was better than the rest of us and never looked down on his teammates—not even on an awestruck rookie linebacker who initially wondered if he belonged in the same locker room with legends like Woodson and Aikman.

My only knock on Aikman—and this is actually a blessing, not a curse—is that he is primarily responsible for one of my only frivolous addictions. I'm a sucker for fast cars and sushi bars, and it was Aikman who first introduced me to the world of sushi. Troy took one of our trainers, Dexter Coakley, and me to a sushi restaurant in Irving one day after practice, and I was hooked from that point forward. Troy picked up the tab that time, but that introduction has cost me hundreds of dollars. On most evenings, Becky and I will bake some chicken or pork at home, put some dressing on top, and that's our dinner. But my weakness is that sushi restaurant in Irving, and I often hear it calling my name. Probably 80 to 90 percent of the time that we do go out, it's there. I have since hooked several of my other teammates, including Dan Campbell, on this particular sushi bar.

But just the mere fact that Aikman would spring for a lunch that included two young linebackers and a trainer says something about his character. He wasn't worried about being seen with the "right" people; he wasn't trying to impress us with his reputation or money; he was just being one of the guys—one of the good guys. I learned a lot by watching some of my teammates during that first NFL season. In watching guys like Woodson and Aikman, I realized you could be a star in this league without letting the fame, the adulation, and the money go to your head. I also probably learned how not to act from a few other team-mates. I watched the way some of my other teammates handled themselves on the field and off and realized I never wanted to be seen in that light. Then I watched how they treated other play-ers, coaches, fans, reporters, and everyone outside their entou-rage, and I vowed never to allow my paycheck, my vehicle, or my wardrobe to dictate my perception of myself or others.

Of course, that's easy for a rookie fighting for his spot on the roster to say, and rest assured, I knew I was fighting for a job. Many of the so-called experts labeled me as an undersized colle-giate inside linebacker, so you can imagine what they were say-ing about my pro potential. Even without reading newspapers I couldn't escape the multitudes of Dat doubters. They were on the local television stations, they called into radio talk shows, and they were all over the Internet. About the nicest thing I heard from the experts early in my rookie season was that I had a chance to be a decent special teams player in the NFL. With Randall Godfrey firmly entrenched as the Cowboys' start-ing middle linebacker, being a regular special teams contributor was my primary goal as a rookie. Besides, I often felt as though I was running around like a chicken with my head cut off on defense during those early two-a-day practices. You can live in the gym, wilt on the track, and watch film until the wee hours of the morning in preparation for the transition to the NFL. But nothing can completely prepare you for the increased speed of the game on the professional level. The college game is played on fast-forward, but the NFL action is played at warp speed. Even the reserve offensive linemen can run, so you better know exactly what you're doing and be moving at full speed on every play in every game and every practice.

I received my first NFL lesson on that subject from a fellow

Aggie, tight end Hayward Clay. During a sweltering two-a-day practice in Wichita Falls, I was covering Clay on a pass route, and I stopped running after him when he caught the pass. As we made our way back to our respective huddles, Clay tapped me on the back and said: "Hey rook, don't ever, ever quit on a play. Not in a game, not in a practice, not even in a drill. Every move you make is taped, analyzed, and scrutinized on this level." Clay's message hit home, and so did the realization that you can't take anything for granted in this league. At its essence, the NFL is still the game you grew up loving and playing for fun. But it's also a monstrous business where the bottom line is always in mind. To turn a profit, owners need to entertain fans. To entertain fans, coaches need to win. To win, players must perform quickly or they will quickly be seeking a new line of work. With a fifty-three-man roster and a sixteen-game schedule, there is little margin for error, little patience for mistakes, and little reason for an undersized, third-round draft pick to breathe easily.

By the time we opened the 1999 preseason schedule on August 9 against Cleveland in the Hall of Fame Game, things were still a bit of a blur. But during that nationally televised game in Canton, Ohio, I did manage to make a few plays at middle linebacker and even recorded a sack, wrapping up Browns rookie quarterback Tim Couch. I still made a boatload of mistakes, but I made enough plays to begin feeling good about my chances of playing at this level. I was also particularly pleased when I received a phone call the next evening from Nancy Bennett.

After Phil Bennett had been fired at A&M following the 1996 season, he had spent one season as the defensive coordinator at TCU and then gone on for the 1998 season as the secondary coach at Oklahoma. Even after he had left A&M, I'd kept in regular contact with Phil, Nancy, and their awesome kids, Sam and Maddi, and I knew Coach Bennett was extremely excited about his new role in 1999 as the defensive coordinator at Kansas State. As I mentioned previously, my bond with Bennett and his family went well beyond the typical player-coach relationship. The Bennetts were like a second family to me, so I was delighted to hear Nancy's vibrant voice following the first preseason game. I was actually with Becky when Nancy called, and we talked for a considerable time. She told me how proud she was of me. She was so excited about my future in the NFL and her family's immediate future at Kansas State. Nancy also told me that she would be following my progress with the Cowboys closely and that she believed in me. We said we would all hook up together—Becky and me, the Bennett kids, and Phil and Nancy—after the end of the season to rekindle old ties and celebrate new beginnings. Then I hung up the phone with a smile on my face because of the way a conversation with Nancy Bennett always made me feel.

Tragically, that was the last conversation Nancy and I ever had. The following morning she awoke early, told Coach Bennett she had talked to me the previous night, and went out for a jog just as she did on virtually every other day. But Nancy never made it back home. She was struck by lightning and then placed on life support for the next seventeen days. She died shortly after Coach Bennett made the agonizing decision to remove her from life support. I really can't even begin to describe just how hard that hit me. I was stunned and in denial when I first heard about it. Later, I grieved for my personal loss. Nancy was my confidante, and I loved her like a family member. But more than the sorrow I was feeling for myself, I grieved for Coach Bennett, Sam, and Maddie. Nancy was just forty-one, and she was the glue that held the Bennett family together. She was vibrant, engaging, nurturing, fun, charismatic, and so much more. Now, in the blink of an eye, she was gone. There are probably at least a handful of defining moments in everyone's life. Nancy Bennett's death was one of mine. I had already vowed to myself to play every down with a sense of purpose and passion—playing every snap as if it was going to be my last. But following Nancy's death, I was also reminded just how important it was to live your life in that same manner. We all know there are no guarantees in this life. But when someone you love and adore is struck down in the prime of her life like Nancy, it's a shocking and sobering reminder of just how fragile life can be.

Following Nancy's death, it was initially tough for me to focus on football. But I talked to Coach Bennett as often as I could, and he reminded me of something I already knew: Nancy would have personally whipped my tail if I had allowed anything to distract me from fulfilling my dreams. With a revitalized focus and a renewed appreciation for the opportunity to follow my dreams, I performed at least fairly well in the preseason and wound up playing on all of the special teams and some of the nickel packages by the time we opened the regular season with an exhilarating 41–35, come-from-behind win over the Washington Redskins. I often felt I was more of a spectator than a participant in that game, but it was a wild way to officially begin your NFL career. We were down 35–14 entering the fourth quarter, and Aikman engineered four scoring drives in the final twenty minutes, including a seventy-six-yard touchdown pass to Raghib "Rocket" Ismail that ended the game in overtime. I made three tackles on special teams and also recovered an onside kick in the fourth quarter that played a key role in the comeback. We also won our next two games to go to 3-0 before losing back-to-back games to the Eagles and Giants by identical 13–10 scores. Many of the professional games run together in my mind as I think back, but I vividly recall the loss to the Giants on Monday Night Football—not because it was nationally televised or because we were on the big stage of the Big Apple, but because of one big block in the back. I was covering a punt, and I was about to make a tackle when I was shoved off course from behind. The punt returner went right past me. As I picked myself up off the ground, I went to the sideline thoroughly disgusted because of the missed tackle. By the time I reached the sideline, however, I heard the official over the loudspeaker say something that brought a wide grin to my face.

"Illegal block in the back, No. 86, on the receiving team," the official said. I started laughing out loud right then. It was Dan Campbell. I couldn't believe Dan had clipped me, but I loved the fact that he got caught. After the game, Dan came over to me and said, "Man, I'm really sorry for blocking you in the back." I told him that wasn't what I had meant when I said to "stay in touch." But we had a good laugh together, and I eventually had the last laugh since we beat the Giants in the final regular season game of the year to slip into the playoffs with an 8-8 record. Once the regular season came to an end, I was stunned at how quickly it had gone by and shocked by how few of the particular moments I could recall.

What's crazy is that I can vividly recall virtually every play of every game while I was in high school and at Texas A&M. The key plays, the scores, the emotions, and the memories are etched permanently and prominently in my mind. But since I've been in the NFL, I sometimes have a difficult time remembering many of the specific events from the previous season—let alone the first season. I think that probably has everything to do with the circumstances surrounding the games. In high school and college, you were surrounded by your buddies, battling for a common cause, and playing for the sheer love of the game. The camaraderie in the high school and college locker rooms is unsurpassed by anything I have ever experienced. It's not the same in the pros. Instead of sharing locker space with guys who are primarily the same age from basically the same region of the country, the NFL locker room brings together men in their mid-thirties with kids fresh out of college. Their priorities are different; their lifestyles and views on life are different; and their personalities can often be much different. You've got established millionaires who have fulfilled most of their dreams in the same space with guys who are scared to death that their dreams may never materialize. The dynamics of that NFL setting make it virtually impossible to ever form the type of close-knit team we had at Texas A&M in 1998.

You do form some bonds inside an NFL locker room, but not nearly as many and, for the most part, not nearly as meaningful as the ones you develop in college or high school. After all, the guys I came in with at Texas A&M were never traded to Baylor or cut off from their scholarship the week before the season began. In the NFL, however, tough personnel issues are part of the business, and business can sometimes be brutally cold. A few mistakes in college could cost you your starting position; a couple of mistakes in the pros can cost you your current ability to put food on your family's table. In other words, there's almost no comparison in terms of the pressure to perform. In all honesty, the business aspect of the professional game takes away some of the fun.

I'm not complaining, and I'm not saying playing professional football isn't a fun way to make a living. It's just not quite as fun as in college or high school. The intense pressure to perform in the NFL changes your perspective on the sport. I have become much more of a perfectionist in the NFL than I ever was in college. During the season and throughout the off-season, I find myself dwelling on the handful of bad plays I made instead of remembering the good ones. During my rookie season, I made eighteen tackles on special teams and another thirty-four on defense. I also recorded one sack, one interception, and one forced fumble and earned a spot on the NFL's All-Rookie team for my work on special teams. But more than any of those plays I made, I remember the ones I missed. I even remember the near mess-ups.

We were terribly inconsistent as a team in 1999, especially on the road. We were 7-1 at home, but 1-7 on the road. The only road game we won all year was in the season opener against the Redskins. Unfortunately, our 8-8 record meant we would have to go on the road in the playoffs as a wild card representative against the Minnesota Vikings. The Vikings outplayed us from start to finish in a 27–10 loss that ended our season. The one thing that really sticks out in my mind about that game was a near nightmare experience. I had just made a tackle while playing middle linebacker, and the coaches were sending in a special "dime" defensive package. But since I was still on the ground after making the tackle, I was late getting toward the sideline. Coach George Edwards yelled to me, "Stay, stay, stay," even though they had five receivers in the formation.

As we lined up, I was trying to convince myself everything would be okay, telling myself, "I know the coverage, I can handle this." I knew there were going to be three receivers to one side and two on the other. My job was to go to the three-receiver side and to make sure the inside receiver didn't run a route to the inside, because there wasn't any help in the secondary. I knew I could do that because Cris Carter was usually the inside receiver, and he would normally do a little three- or five-yard out. But when I actually lined up and looked up, the inside receiver was Vikings superstar Randy Moss. I don't know if Moss heard me, but I specifically remember uttering the words "Uh, oh." I looked back hoping to see some deep help in the secondary, but there wasn't any. I thought to myself, "Man, if he catches the ball, it's going to be da-da-da, da-da-da. It's going to be ESPN highlight reel material." I was still thinking he was going to run a three-yard out, but when the ball was snapped, Moss started running in place, and I was thinking, "What the heck?" Then I thought that maybe it was a delayed out. So I jumped to the outside to defend the out route. Instead, he turned back inside and was going on the slant. My first thought then was, "Oh, my gosh. I'm toast, and he's going to score if he catches this thing." I had to do something quickly because I was beat. So, I stuck my foot out and tripped him. He fell down, but none of the officials saw me trip him. I initially felt as though I should apologize to him, but Randy just got up, tapped me on the head, and said, "Nice move."

It was also an illegal move, but it saved my butt and knocked Moss on his. It wasn't pretty, but I got the job done. I could probably say the same thing for my entire rookie season. It wasn't always pretty, but I most often got the job done and learned so much about what it takes to make it in the NFL. When the season finally came to an end in early January of 2000, I was mentally and physically drained. The most games I had ever played in a season prior to 1999 was the fourteen we played at Texas A&M in 1998 en route to winning the Big 12 championship. But even with fourteen, there were some breaks along the way, including a three-week layoff between the title game and the Sugar Bowl. But in 1999, the Cowboys played twenty-two games (including the preseason and the playoffs) in twenty-three weeks. It takes a toll on your body and your mind, especially since I had basically been going nonstop in terms of training, practicing, and preparing for the next season since my junior year in college. So, after the 1999 season, Becky and I decided to celebrate my first year in the NFL and her graduation from A&M by going to Cabo San Lucas. It was an awesome trip until we learned that my aunt, to whom I was extremely close, had died in a car wreck in Rockport.

Death is obviously a part of life, and it is something that will directly and indirectly affect us all. But in a matter of months, I had lost two of the more meaningful women in my life—Nancy Bennett and my Aunt Mai—to freakish accidents. Dealing with such shocking, unexpected news was naturally difficult. I think those events only made me more focused on the most important things in my life—my faith in Jesus Christ, my growing relationship with Becky, and my football career. I also made a conscious effort not to put off until tomorrow what I could do today. After all, there are no guarantees a tomorrow will ever come. In the aftermath of my rookie season and my aunt's funeral, I realized God had blessed me with an incredible woman—the woman of my dreams—and an incredible opportunity to live out my dreams as a professional football player. In my own mind, I decided it was time to make sure I made the most of those blessings.

I worked extremely hard during the off-season of 2000, hoping the extra workouts would help me break into the starting lineup. Chan Gailey was fired as the head coach following the '99 season, and he was replaced by Dave Campo, our former defensive coordinator. I liked Campo a lot, and I knew he was in my corner. I knew Campo believed I could be a starter, and when Randall Godfrey signed a monstrous, $25 million deal with the Tennessee Titans during the off-season, I knew the door to the starting lineup was wide open for me.

On the personal side, I also knew another door was open, so to speak. I was convinced beyond any doubt that I wanted to marry Becky. We had gone through so many ups and downs and had seen our relationship endure break-ups, separations, and virtually everything else. After I was drafted by the Cowboys and first moved to Dallas to begin working out with the team, I would drive to College Station after Friday workouts to spend the weekend with Becky. I would then drive back to Dallas at 5:00 a.m. on Monday so that I could be at workouts by 9:00 a.m. Yes, I know it would have been much easier to drive back on Sunday evening, but spending every extra minute with Becky was well worth the early wake-up calls. When we were apart, I pictured myself with her, and I absolutely couldn't picture a future without her.

I had already been formulating some engagement plans in my mind. I knew we would be in Denver for a game on August 19 during the 2000 preseason. I picked out a ring from a jewelry store in Colorado and arranged for the ring to be sent to my cousin who lived in Denver. Then I planned to get the ring from him following our game against the Broncos. My cousin had other plans. He came down to the railing along the bottom of the stadium just after halftime and told me he was going to leave early. He then gave me the engagement ring. It was a preseason game, so I was done playing by halftime, but I was still thinking, "What am I going to do with this ring right now? What if someone gets hurt and I have to go back in the game?" I could just see myself having to ask one of our assistant coaches, "Do you mind holding this little box for me? Please hold onto it very carefully, because it just happens to be the most important purchase of my life." I could also visualize Dave Campo getting wind of such an item. *"Dat, I thought you were focused on being the starting middle linebacker for the Dallas Cowboys. You should be thinking about winning a ring, son, not buying one during the game."*

Fortunately, none of my backups were injured during the second half, and I never needed to go back into the game. I kept the ring box wrapped in a towel and stuffed into my helmet. And you can bet that I never let go of my helmet until the game ended and we were back in the locker room. We flew back to Dallas that evening, and during the flight, I began formulating my proposal plans. I knew Becky was not suspecting this anytime soon. She knew it would eventually come, and we had even talked about getting married. But now that the season had started, I knew she wouldn't be expecting anything until at least after the season. But the Denver game signified the end of two-a-days, and instead of going back to Wichita Falls, we would stay in Dallas as we prepared for our final preseason game. As I went through proposal ideas in my mind, I decided I would pop the question on her birthday, August 30. But when the plane landed in Dallas, my plans soon went awry. One of the things I love most about Becky is that we share everything with each other. I have a really hard time keeping things from her, and she usually sees right through me.

So, on August 20—my first full day back from training camp—Becky and I went to McDonald's for our usual shake. She later told me she knew something was out of the ordinary when I ordered us large milkshakes instead of our standard small ones. She said I seemed to be acting a little strange, that I didn't seem like myself. I knew I could never keep this up for ten more days, so we went home, and I asked her to join me on the back porch. I think I told her that I wanted to share our shake on the back porch for a change of pace, which only made me look more weird. But when I got down on one knee in front of her and opened the box, she understood I wasn't just being weird; I was being the hopeless romantic that I am. Some guys spend thousands of dollars—in addition to the cost of the ring—simply arranging the perfect proposal. I spent a couple bucks on milkshakes. But as I said before, I'm rarely extravagant, usually simplistic, and typically frugal. At least I sprang for large milkshakes. Another thing I love about Becky is that she says it was the perfect proposal for her. We don't need fireworks going off in the backyard or an orchestra playing in the background—not even for a moment like that. She burst into tears when I got down on a knee, and she said yes to my proposal, officially making me the luckiest man on the planet.

Fortunately, I was lucky at love, because my luck wasn't so good at football. I made the first official start of my pro football career on September 3 against the Philadelphia Eagles. It was blisteringly hot, with the temperature at kickoff rising to 109. The thermometer on Texas Stadium's artificial turf topped out at 170. But we were even uglier than we were hot. Troy Aikman was sacked three times early in the game and left the contest about three minutes into the second quarter with a concussion. Later in the game, wide receiver Joey Galloway was carted off the field after tearing the ACL in his left knee. The Cowboys had given up two first-round draft picks in a trade with Seattle to acquire Galloway, who was projected to be Michael Irvin's replacement. Irvin had been forced to retire after a serious neck injury during the '99 season. But one game into the season, we had lost Galloway for the year, and Aikman's status was in serious question. Without Aikman and Galloway, we lost, 41–14. To add insult to the injuries, we allowed Duce Staley to rush for 201 yards, the first person to rush for more than 200 yards against the Cowboys since 1984. In fact, we allowed 306 total rushing yards, the most in Cowboys history. I managed eight tackles and intercepted a pass, but it wasn't nearly enough to prevent a lopsided loss.

It turned out to be an ominous beginning to a disheartening season. Aikman played in only eleven games in 2000 because of injuries, and he was forced to retire at the end of the year. And Troy wasn't the only one who was banged up again and again. In the second game of the season—a 32–31 loss at Arizona—I sprained the MCL in my left knee and was forced to sit out the next three games. Once I returned to action in a 19–14 loss to the New York Giants, I sustained some nerve damage in my neck during the fourth quarter and again had to sit out the next three games. My neck would continue to bother me throughout the rest of the season, but I did come back to play the final seven games of the year.

I regained my starting position for the final two weeks of the season and finished the year with sixty-four tackles and two interceptions. But the statistic the media focused on the most was the number six—as in six games missed due to injuries. It was bad enough that we went 5-11 and finished twenty-second in the league—out of thirty-one teams—in scoring defense. But it was all made worse by the constant chorus of "I told you so" theories regarding my injuries. Whenever I turned on the television or radio, I was floored by the number of people who were already convinced that I would never be able to be a consistent starter in the NFL because of my lack of size. The 2000 season, the skeptics claimed, was proof of that.

Nothing fuels me like the challenge of someone telling me I can't do something. I love to challenge myself, but I especially like to prove people wrong when they underestimate me. And, of course, this certainly wasn't the first time I had heard that I was too small to play. I wouldn't be surprised if the words "too small" follow me all the way to the grave and wind up etched onto my tombstone—right next to the words, "Pronounced 'Win.'" But I knew my injuries weren't a result of being too small; they were simply a matter of being in the wrong position at the wrong time. Besides, after two seasons in the NFL, there was no longer any doubt in my mind that I could play at this level.

I took some time off following the conclusion of the 2000 season to rest, relax, . . . and eventually rejoice. While the 2000 football season was filled with frustrating moments, the ensuing off-season was filled with exhilarating ones. On March 10, 2001, Becky and I were married at St. Mary's Catholic Church in College Station. It was a small, intimate wedding with only family and a select number of friends. But we had such a good time that we decided to do it again and again. After we returned from our honeymoon, we were married again in a traditional Vietnamese wedding in Rockport, where we probably had about five hundred people in attendance. Then one week later, we went to Becky's hometown in Runge for a reception with her family and friends. So when it was all said and done, we had two weddings and three receptions. It was actually a little tiring, but it was certainly memorable.

Then it was back to work in preparation for the 2001 season. I studied hard, worked hard, lifted hard, and ran hard. I believed I had something to prove during the 2001 season, and, as a team, we believed we were on the verge of turning a corner. Unfortunately, we turned the corner and ran into a brick wall. We lost our first four games in 2001 and were only 2-8 late in the year. We finished the year at 5-11 for the second consecutive time and missed the playoffs once again. It was very disappointing, but from an individual standpoint, the 2001 season was a breakthrough year for me. I opened the season with a career-best 15 tackles against Tampa Bay and played well throughout the first month of the season. Even when I did endure an injury, I played through the pain. I dislocated my ring finger on my right hand against the Eagles on September 30, and I had to have surgery to place a pin in the finger on October 1. But I never missed a game. The following week—with a huge cast on my right hand—I had eight tackles at Oakland. By the time the season ended, I had started all sixteen games and recorded 172 tackles—the second-best single-season total in the history of the Dallas Cowboys behind Eugene Lockhart's record-setting year in 1989. I led the team in tackles eleven times and also recorded double-digit tackles eleven times. More significantly to me, I helped our defense finish fourth overall in the NFL rankings by allowing just 287.4 yards per game. We allowed 927 fewer rushing yards than the previous season, which represented the largest turnaround by any defensive unit in the NFL in 2001.

It was, far and away, my best season in the NFL. I joked with Becky after the season, telling her that I probably should have put a ring on her finger a couple of years earlier because it was obvious that married life was good for me. But in all sincerity, I did feel particularly lucky and extremely blessed following the 2001 season. On the field, I was no longer being viewed as part of the problem but rather as part of the future solution. At home, things couldn't have been any better. Things were going so well that I was almost tempted to do something outlandishly out of character for me—something like walking into one of my favorite restaurants and ordering an entire round of drinks for everyone on me. But then I came to my senses and decided against such a foolish notion. After all, they don't give those milkshakes away at McDonald's.

CHAPTER 12

The Ride of My Life

A CAREER IN THE NATIONAL FOOTBALL LEAGUE can be like taking an elevator ride in one of those gigantic, upscale hotels. You have a destination in mind, but how long it actually takes you to get there can depend completely on the people who are sharing the ride. And although those people may be cordial to you while you are together, no one really cares if you step off on the wrong floor. The elevator will continue with or without you. If you punch the right buttons, it can take you to the top, where the view is spectacular and the amenities are all first-rate. But even if you make it to the top for an extended stay in the penthouse, you will eventually come down. Everyone does. Then, once you reach the bottom, a new set of riders is anxiously waiting for you to get the heck out of the way so that they can take their ride to the top.

A significant difference, of course, is that an elevator ride is usually quite predictable and safe. The up-and-down nature of life in the NFL, on the other hand, can often be as unpredictable and dangerous as maneuvering through motorists in rush-hour traffic. In the NFL you can seemingly be cruising along the fast lane of success when, out of nowhere, someone blindsides you. Your plans, your season, and possibly even your career can come crashing to a halt in the blink of an eye. That's a humbling and rather cruel reality. From an emotional standpoint, it's like taking an express elevator ride from the penthouse to the rock-bottom basement level.

I experienced both the highs and lows of that elevator ride during the off-season in 2002. After what I considered a break-through season in 2001, I was entering the final year of my contract in 2002. I was well aware of the Cowboys' recent history in dealing with linebackers, allowing talented and productive guys like Ken Norton, Jr., Darren Smith, Dixon Edwards, Robert Jones, and Randall Godfrey to sign with other teams instead of locking them in to long-term contracts. So, I knew there was a distinct possibility that 2002 could be my final season in Dallas. But I also had a strong desire to stay with the Cowboys, and after some negotiations, my agent and Cowboys C.O.O. Stephen Jones reached a deal.

For as long as he has been the owner of the Cowboys, Jerry Jones has been the frequent target of media criticism. I suppose it comes with the territory, although what I know is that Jones built a franchise that won three Super Bowls in a span of four years. In the twenty-nine years before Jones became the owner, the Cowboys had won two Super Bowls. In my book, that makes him one of the elite owners in the professional sports world. From my personal dealings with him, I have nothing but the utmost respect for Jerry Jones. He's a marketing machine, an innovative entrepreneur, and a shrewd businessman. He's made some difficult and unpopular decisions that have drawn harsh criticism from the media, but that's the nature of the NFL beast. In all likelihood, there will come a day when Jones will be required to make a business decision that ends my playing days with the Cowboys. But even when that day comes, I will have nothing but good things to say about him. He's been great for the Dallas Cowboys, and he has been very good to me.

I will always be grateful to Jones for drafting me, and I will especially be grateful to him for giving me the opportunity to stay in Dallas. I really enjoy living in the Dallas–Fort Worth area, and I love the idea of possibly being able to play my entire football career—high school, college, and professional—in the state of Texas. Jones gave me that kind of opportunity with my second contract. He didn't have to do it. He could have simply allowed me to play out the final year of my contract and either negotiated with me then or let me go. Instead, Jones showed his trust in me and signed me to a six-year, multimillion-dollar contract on April 16, 2002. It wasn't what some guys might consider a mega-bucks contract, but it meant the world to me. When Becky and I left the press conference announcing the deal, I felt both extraordinarily motivated to prove to the Cowboys that they had made the right move and incredibly blessed because of our new financial stability.

I grew up in a comfortable home, and I even had my own room in the last house my parents built. It was so small that I could practically sit in the middle of my room and touch all four walls without getting up. Some people might have labeled it a closet instead of a bedroom, but thanks to my parents' tireless efforts, I never lacked for anything I needed. On the other hand, the words "disposable income" were not part of our family's vocabulary. My father rarely brought up Vietnam to his children, but when I drifted into my adolescent lazy mode, he would remind me that when he was eleven, he had worked all day collecting, carrying, and selling bamboo in hopes of making fifty cents' worth of profit, which he had then turned over to my grandfather. Even when my parents began to see some of the fruits of their labor in the restaurant business in Rockport-Fulton, they pinched pennies to make ends meet. They also instilled in my siblings and me a sincere appreciation for every hard-earned dollar that came into our home. So, to be able to sign a multi-year, multimillion dollar contract to play football was a blessing beyond what I ever would have imagined as a youngster.

Growing up, I figured I would follow in my family's footsteps, working shrimp boats along the Gulf Coast or serving shrimp dishes. I'm certain I could have been happy in a job like that, but unless my shrimp nets had somehow uncovered the lost treasures of the Gulf, I'm also certain I never would have seen a seven-figure income. Not in one lump sum, not in a year, and probably not in a lifetime. Football has obviously taken me places and afforded me opportunities I never would have thought possible.

After signing the deal with Dallas, I wanted to show my appreciation to the Cowboys by making a commitment to work harder during the rest of the off-season than I ever had before. Now, the word "off-season" is actually outdated. It implies that you take time off once the season is completed. Because of the caliber of athletes in the NFL today, you simply can't afford to take much time off. You must stay in shape twelve months out of the year to stay in the league. Realizing that, I had always stayed in shape during my first three seasons in the league. But I was now driven to take things to another level to prove the Cowboys were justified in putting their future hopes at middle linebacker in me.

When the 2002 season began, I felt better than I ever had as an athlete. I had actually trimmed down a little bit to 235 pounds, but I was stronger than ever. During my weight workouts prior to the 2002 season, I maxed out at just over 500 pounds in the bench press. I was also running as well as ever, and, as a three-year veteran in the NFL coming off my best season yet, I had a better understanding of what it took to excel at this level. Quite frankly, I was anticipating a monster year, and I was extremely excited about opening the season in Houston against the expansion Texans. I had numerous friends and family members in the stands, and I was in the best physical shape of my life. As I stood on the sidelines of the sparkling new Reliant Stadium prior to the kickoff, I felt as though I was in the penthouse enjoying the view. Then that express elevator picked me up and dropped me down.

On the first defensive series of the game, I came on a blitz up the middle. It was a crisscross blitz with Dexter Coakley and me. The idea was for Dexter to go first and serve as a decoy so that I could go free to the quarterback. The offensive guard picked up Dexter, and I thought I was about to get to Texans quarterback David Carr. Just before I reached him, the running back came out of nowhere, hitting me right on top of my right wrist with his helmet. I immediately felt a sharp pain, but I certainly didn't think it was any big deal. Even if you watched the tape of the game looking for that particular play, you wouldn't think anything of it. It looks like a normal hit, and I figured at the time that the pain would go away in a few seconds.

I figured wrong. When I went to the sideline, I put my hand on the bench and began pressing down to see if my wrist was okay. The sound it made resembled what you might hear if someone was chomping on a bag of tortilla chips. I knew right away the wrist was broken, and when I showed it to Dexter, he said my hand looked as though it was hanging by only a few threads off the end of my arm. "You need to keep your butt on that bench and stay out of this game," Dexter said. "That thing looks bad."

It was bad, but I had so much adrenaline going through my veins that I decided I could continue playing. I had the trainers tape my wrist up and provide me with some pain killers so I could play the rest of the game. In hindsight, I'm not really sure how I did it, but I played the rest of the game and had a team-high eleven tackles with one sack and a tackle for a loss.

But here's a little word to the wise youngsters who may be reading this book: Dexter was right; I shouldn't have played the rest of the game. I had worked so hard and felt so good that I was determined not to leave my teammates out there without me. But in playing the rest of the game, I did further damage to my wrist. When the doctors examined the X-rays the next day the surgeon said I had one of the worst breaks he had ever seen. In fact, he said he had seen similar breaks only in bull riders who'd had their wrists trampled on by thirteen-hundred-pound bulls.

Immediate surgery was required, and I went under the knife that Monday night—some twenty-four hours after our season-opening loss to the Texans. This was definitely not the way I had envisioned things happening. I honestly thought we were going to be a much-improved football team, but we managed to lose to an expansion franchise on national television. That was rather humbling. And on a personal level, I was initially very disappointed. I was looking forward to the best season of my life. Instead, I was on an operating table about to have pins placed in my wrist. The surgery was so complicated and intricate—and the stitches were so numerous and long—that doctors told me I couldn't even sweat while my wrist was recovering. Do you know how difficult it is not to sweat living in Dallas, Texas, during the month of September? "C'mon," I told the doctors, "you can work up a sweat driving on 635 in an air-conditioned car." But they were serious, and for the next six to eight weeks I was instructed not to sweat. Among other things, that meant no lifting weights with my upper body, no exercising outside, and no more "prime physical condition." The doctors estimated that I would miss at least six to eight games, and I wondered what kind of shape I would be in even when I did make it back to action.

The injury also added fuel to the fire of all the critics who sang the refrain of "Dat's too small to take the constant pounding." I ignored that as much as possible, but I could not ignore the fact that most of my hopes and dreams for the season had been dashed in the blink of an eye and the break of a wrist. It was not career-threatening, and it wasn't even season-ending, but it was tough to take. I have, however, lived my Christian life under the premise of "everything happens for a reason." I say those words to myself as often as I mention them to others. I sincerely believe everything that happens is part of God's master plan for our lives, including the disappointments, the adverse circumstances, and the bad breaks that inevitably occur in everyone's life. After initially feeling a little sorry for myself because of my injury, I decided that now was a prime time to determine my level of spiritual maturity. Was I going to continue feeling sorry for myself, dwelling on opportunities lost and negative remarks from the media? Or was I going to face this injury with a positive attitude, placing complete faith that everything was going to work out for the best in God's plans?

I decided the latter was clearly the best option, and some amazing things began to happen. I really felt an incredible peace of mind about my career and came to the realization that there was no point in sweating what you couldn't control. Of course, with this particular injury, there was also no sweating at all. I did manage to keep in moderately decent shape by doing some squats and lower-body exercises and even running a little on an indoor treadmill. Just before I would break into a sweat, however, I would have to stop and "cool it," so to speak. I also did some soul-searching during that time regarding the overall direction of my life. I was about to celebrate my twenty-seventh birthday, and as I pondered my immediate future and a future beyond football, I became more and more mesmerized by the thought of having children. I could live happily ever after without football;

I could easily picture Becky and me with a much more modest lifestyle; but I had a more difficult time imagining us spending the rest of our lives together without children.

We both love and adore children. As I have pointed out, we consider ourselves two children in adult bodies. From the time our dating relationship began to get more serious, Becky and I would talk about how many children we would like to have, what they might look like, the list of possible names, and so forth. Now we were both ready to begin building a family of our own. But it was not as easy as we had hoped. We had been trying to conceive for about nine months prior to my injury, and while I certainly enjoyed the "practice," our lack of reproductive success was frustrating. Many of our couples friends had told us about how easy it was for them to get pregnant, which made our difficulties even more disappointing. Becky went to the doctor, who informed us there were some fertility issues and that we would probably not be able to conceive in a traditional manner. It was difficult news to hear. We talked about adopting, and we discussed going to some fertility specialists. But ultimately, we decided to give it to God and pray about it before taking any other action.

You know that thing I said earlier about everything happens for a reason? Well, when I was forced to stay indoors and curtail my workouts because of my injured wrist, Becky and I had even more time together. And on October 1, 2002, I received the most pleasant surprise of my life. Earlier in the day, Becky had been at a little shop where she did some part-time work with a friend. The owner of the shop had a little boy who was four months old, and for some reason, Becky just couldn't let go of the little boy. She just wanted to hold him and love on him—even more than she normally would, which is saying a lot. So, she came home that evening and—unknown to me—decided to take a pregnancy test. It was positive. But with her doctor's words ringing in her ears, Becky didn't believe it. So she took another one. And another one. And just to be absolutely sure, she took one more. Four tests, four positive results. It seemed a little strange to me when, out of the blue, she told me that she needed to go to the grocery store that evening. I asked her if it couldn't wait until the next day, and she quickly said no. Then I asked her what she needed, and she muttered several things. So we hopped in the car, pulled into the parking lot of the nearby Tom Thumb Grocery Store, and she made a beeline to the greeting card aisle.

To be perfectly honest, I was getting a little annoyed at this point, since she hadn't mentioned a card on her impromptu shopping list. I wasn't really paying attention to the type of cards she was looking for, but I was fussing at her, saying things like, "Don't you think it might be time for us to get the things you actually said we had to come here tonight to get?" Finally, Becky spotted the perfect card and slipped something out of her pocket and into the card. She then handed it to me. I opened it and saw the positive test results, and, in the middle of the Tom Thumb card aisle, we began whooping and hollering in joyous celebration. We were going to have a baby! I was so excited that I was a little concerned I might break into a full sweat.

That little piece of news changes your perspective on everything, and I am pretty sure the smile didn't leave my face until I finally was cleared by the doctors to return to practice in mid-November. When I did get back in a game on November 17 in Indianapolis, we were 3-6 and teetering on the edge of playoff elimination. We lost to the Colts, 20–3, which all but eliminated us from the playoff picture for a third consecutive season. We won the next two games against Jacksonville and Washington, but we closed the season on a four-game losing skid. We were once again 5-11, which led Jerry Jones to fire Dave Campo.

Personally, I always liked Coach Campo, and to this day, I think he has an outstanding defensive mind. But in three seasons as head coach, Campo compiled a 15-33 record and became the first coach in team history to produce three consecutive seasons with ten or more losses. Campo had come to the Cowboys with Jimmy Johnson, starting as a defensive assistant, then becoming the defensive coordinator in 1995 when Butch Davis left for the head coaching position at the University of Miami. Campo was an outstanding defensive coordinator, but it just didn't work out for him as a head coach. Most of the players genuinely liked him, but I'm not sure if Coach Campo ever commanded the amount of respect from the entire locker room that he needed in order to be a successful head coach.

The man who replaced him, on the other hand, certainly did. On January 2, 2003, Jones and the Cowboys officially introduced Bill Parcells as the head coach. Like practically every other football fan in the country, I knew about Parcells' legendary reputation as a no-nonsense, results-oriented, hard-driving coaching machine. I also knew that his track record with the New York Giants, New England Patriots, and New York Jets was remarkable. The Giants were 4-5 in the strike-shortened season before Parcells took over in 1983. They made the playoffs his second season and won the Super Bowl in his fourth and eighth seasons. In New England, he took a team that was 2-14 before his arrival and led them to the playoffs in his second season. They reached the Super Bowl in his fourth season. Then he guided the Jets from 1-15 in the season before he made it to the AFC title game two years later. In my four professional seasons, on the other hand, I had yet to play on a team that finished the year with a winning record. So, I was obviously excited about the news of Parcells' arrival. I didn't know the secret of his success or anything else about him. But I knew he was a winner, and I definitely wanted to be part of a winning franchise.

What I learned in the aftermath of his hiring, however, was that part of Parcells' past recipe for success had been not to go to battle with linebackers like me. I can't even begin to tell you how many times—from the day Parcells was hired in January until we began the 2003 season in September—Dexter Coakley and I heard we were not "Parcells-type linebackers." In his previous coaching stops he had utilized much bigger linebackers like Harry Carson, Pepper Johnson, George Martin, Carl Banks, Vincent Brown, Mo Lewis, and Marvin Jones as anchors in the middle of his defense. Almost immediately following the hiring of Parcells, people began speculating whether I was going to be traded, cut, or relegated to backup duty on the bench. I can honestly say that none of the speculation fazed me in the least. I couldn't control my size. I wasn't suddenly going to grow three inches and add twenty pounds. But I knew I could play in the NFL, and I was convinced that if Coach Parcells gave me a chance, I could prove my worth to him.

Despite playing with a monstrous cast around my right wrist, I finished the 2003 season in strong fashion. I could barely even grab people with my right hand, but I finished the year by making seventy tackles in the final seven games. I was also voted by my teammates as the recipient of the Ed Block Courage Award for the way I played after coming back from the surgery. So even if I didn't pan out as a Parcells guy, I believed I could play somewhere. Of course, I wasn't going to jump to any conclusions. I wanted to see what made Parcells tick, I wanted to be part of a turnaround in Dallas, and I wanted to see if I could fit into his future plans. And the first time I met Parcells I received the strong sense that he would give me a fair shot. I was also 100 percent convinced that he would not base any of his personnel decisions on media speculation.

I was on the treadmill at the Cowboys' practice facility in Valley Ranch in early January, when Parcells walked in and began talking to another player about losing weight. Parcells told him he'd better lose the weight because the only fat guy who was going to be sticking around was him. I was trying not to show I was listening, but I was. Parcells then came over to me, and we talked for a little bit while I was speed-walking on the treadmill. He told me we had a mutual friend in R. C. Slocum, and he made some other small talk. But then he point-blank asked me, "Are you lazy?" I told him I wasn't, and he said, "Good, because if you are lazy, you aren't going to like it around here. But if you're willing to put in the work, you'll be fine." I got the message, and I was certainly willing to do whatever it took to prove to Parcells that I could be the exception to his "big linebackers are better" rule. From our initial conversations, I also got the sense that I could really enjoy playing for him.

Before Parcells arrived, there was a sense of apathy in our locker room and definitely a lack of football focus. Some people were still living off the Super Bowl years of the '90s, and some were more interested in making a buck than making a play. We had all sorts of people coming in and out of the locker room at all times, selling shoes and clothes, pitching business ideas, and so forth. When Parcells came in, he made it clear there were to be no visitors and no business deals in the locker room. He ripped posters and press clippings off the walls and turned down the air-conditioning to fifty degrees in the training room. He also prohibited eating in the training room. The point was clear: he didn't want anybody to be lounging or enjoying his time in the training room. If you were injured seriously enough, you could endure the cold. If you weren't, you needed to be on the field. He put his foot down and immediately set the tone for the way things would be conducted under his charge.

As I watched him work, I was more and more impressed with how meticulous he is in his attention to detail and how brilliantly he reads people. You really don't want to talk to him more than five minutes at a time, because he will start throwing stuff out from left field to see how you respond to him and to assess how smart you are. He also likes to begin conversations with you to see how committed you are to the team. When we lift weights, we would be on the clock for two minutes in between power cleans and bench presses. Parcells would strike up a conversation with a guy solely to see if he would continue paying attention to his workouts and the clock or if he would chit-chat as long as Parcells stuck around. Parcells believes that if you talk to him longer than two minutes, you are more likely to talk big than to play big. If he can't trust you to keep your focus in the weight room, he won't be able to trust you in the fourth quarter.

Virtually everything Parcells does or says around the team is a calculated move, designed to expose a weakness, determine a player's toughness, or give his team an edge. After just a few weeks of being around him, it was easy to see why he is so successful. He doesn't tolerate dumb mistakes on the field—like jumping offsides, holding, or forgetting assignments. Nor does he tolerate being late for meetings or practices, being lazy, or being out of shape. And anyone who thinks he may be bigger than the team is in for some big surprises with Parcells in charge. He can be intimidating, demanding, motivating, and cunning, but more than anything else, he is the master of preparing. He's the only coach I've ever been around who, in addition to breaking down his own team and the opponents, also breaks down the officials. He studies and evaluates every NFL crew. Before each game, Parcells will tell us in advance the crew's tendencies, what the officials might not call, what they called the week before, and what they called earlier in the season. No stone is ever left unturned with Bill Parcells.

We also practice for situations that most coaches would never even imagine. If those situations come up in a game, we're ready for them. After we lost our first game of the 2003 season in very disappointing fashion to Atlanta, we built a 29–14 lead over the New York Giants early in the fourth quarter the next week. The Giants scored the next 18 points to take a 32–29 lead with eleven seconds left in the game. The Giants kicked the ball out of bounds on the ensuing kickoff, giving us the ball at our own forty with time for only one or two more plays. Most teams probably would have just run a Hail Mary or two and hoped for the best. But we already knew exactly what we would do because we had practiced for this precise situation. We threw a twenty-six-yard pass that got the ball out of bounds at the Giants' thirty-four and then kicked a fifty-two-yard field goal on the last play of regulation to tie the game. We then won the game in overtime, proving to everyone on our roster that Parcells was, indeed, a situational genius. From then on, everybody on our team didn't just believe in Parcells; we all had complete faith in him. We knew we weren't that much more talented than we had been when we were going 5-11 three straight seasons, but we believed we had an edge in Parcells. I don't think the man ever sleeps, which is probably why his teams rarely appear to be sleepwalking. No situation ever arose that we were surprised by or unprepared to handle.

Following that season-opening loss, we won seven of our next eight games and then finished the regular season with a 10-6 record, which was good enough to put us back in the playoffs for the first time since 1999. It's obviously much more fun to win, but it was especially enjoyable to see how Parcells molded a team of modest talent into a cohesive unit that at one point in late November had the best record in the NFC. We didn't finish the job and failed to win the NFC East. We also lost in the first round of the playoffs to a team—the Carolina Panthers—that went on to play in the Super Bowl. Nevertheless, the 2003 season was, in hindsight, a terrific first step in rebuilding the image of the Dallas Cowboys. I was amazed at just how much of an edge Parcells had provided us in only a year's time. He instilled a toughness in our team that didn't exist prior to his arrival. In turn, I think we began to reflect his discipline and hard-nosed personality in the way we fought and scraped out wins. He made the game more fun and far more satisfying than any other year I had played in the NFL, as we finished the season as the top-ranked defense in the league. I can speak only for myself, but it obviously didn't take me long to become sold on Bill Parcells.

Contrary to all the speculation before the 2003 season, I think I also made a believer out of Parcells. I started all seventeen games (including the playoff game) and finished the season with a team-high 132 tackles, including two sacks, two forced fumbles, two fumble recoveries, eight quarterback pressures, and ten passes defended. I was named to the All-Pro second team and was chosen as an alternate to the Pro Bowl. Prior to a mid-November game against New England, Parcells referred to me as a "football-playing dude" to the media, a phrase that definitely received plenty of play. He later said that, while he still preferred bigger linebackers, I could have played and excelled in any of the defensive units he had ever assembled. That would place me in pretty elite company. Considering all the skeptical remarks that had been made about my not being a Bill Parcells type of linebacker, it was nice to hear those comments coming from one of the true all-time legends in the coaching profession.

I have been called a lot of things during my athletic career, dating all the way back to the not-so-affectionate terms I heard on the soccer fields during times of racial unrest in Rockport. I have also been compared to some of the people I most admire in the NFL's past and present—guys like Lee Roy Jordan, Mike Singletary, and Zach Thomas. Throughout my career, I have received more than my fair share of praise and glowing compliments from coaches, opponents, teammates, and reporters. Some of it has been unwarranted, undeserved, and overwhelming. Perhaps some of the criticisms for supposedly being too small have been un-merited, as well. But of all the things that have been said about me through the years, the comments from Parcells were some of the most meaningful in terms of my football career. Yet I can honestly say that Parcells' compliments were not *the* most mean-ingful words I heard during 2003. Not even close, as a matter of fact.

Following the completion of my fifth year in the NFL, some people said that 2003 was the best year of my career. It was actu-ally the best year of my life even before the season ever began. At 4:04 a.m. on June 26, 2003, Becky delivered our daughter, Aubrey Mai Nguyen, who is named after my aunt who died in a car accident following the conclusion of the 1999 season. Aside from the words "I do" which Becky uttered in 2000, the sweet-est, most meaningful words I had ever heard at that point in my life were said by a doctor in the delivery room. I was too weak in the knees at the time of Aubrey's birth to recite the doctor's ex-act words now, but as he handed her to Becky, he said something like, "Mom, Dad, here's your beautiful little girl."

I could have melted, and I couldn't have agreed with him more. Even though she looked just like me and was still a little dis-torted and discolored from the delivery, she was—next to her mother—the most beautiful thing I had ever seen. When I held her in my arms for the first time, I was overcome with gratitude and struck by the realization of what a miraculous journey God has enabled me to make. And as I write this book, my gratitude is compounded as we await the miracle of our second child's birth in July of 2005. The word "miracle" is thrown around too often in the sports world and in our everyday life. Although I've flip-pantly said it a few times, it's not a miracle when you don't get caught in traffic on 635. Nor is it a miracle when a game-winning pass is completed in the back of the end zone on the final play of the contest. Unusual, yes. Exciting, sure. But not miraculous.

What is miraculous to me is to be able to walk into my sleeping child's room each night, brush back her hair, and kiss the forehead of an angel God has so generously loaned to me. According to the doctors, we weren't supposed to be able to have Aubrey. Nor were we supposed to be able to have any other children. But then again, I wasn't supposed to be here, either. According to Ho Chi Minh and the leaders of the North Vietnamese Army, my parents were supposed to stay in Vietnam, surrendering their freedoms, their faith, and their family members to the Communist movement. For every one of my immediate family members to escape from a war-torn country and to find safe passage first to Thailand—eluding the Thai pirates for a month at sea—and then to the United States is miraculous. And then for the baby my mother carried in her womb during that harrowing journey to grow to be big enough to play America's favorite game on some of this country's biggest stages is, in a word, miraculous.

I only hope that my children can one day fully appreciate the incredible odds their grandparents courageously faced to make possible the life they now enjoy. I hope my kids will never be forced to flee from their country, establish roots in a foreign land, or encounter racism so intense that their lives—and the lives of their loved ones—are threatened. But if they ever do face those or similarly difficult obstacles, they should take comfort in the fact that they possess some of the same courageous genes as their grandparents, who were perfectly willing to risk their lives so that their children might live life to the fullest. My parents may be small in stature, but they are uncommonly large role models to me and my siblings. One of the most memorable moments of my life was the day I watched my mom and dad hold Aubrey for the first time. They didn't say much, but I could tell by the glow in their eyes and the smiles on their faces that they, too, were at least briefly taken aback by the number of miraculous events that took place to bring Aubrey, as well as their other grandchildren, into this world. My parents are true heroes, and I am grateful to them for instilling in me the beliefs that hard work can overcome hard times; that faith can move mountains; and that risking death in pursuit of your dreams is far better than living without them.

That's quite an inheritance I received from my parents—one far more valuable than any dollar amount and one that I hope to pass along to my kids. Of course, our children are also blessed with their mother's side of the genetic pool. Becky's parents, Kenneth and Myrna Foster, are two of the kindest, most warm-hearted people I have ever come across. From the first time I ever met them, they accepted me into their family with open arms. And they obviously did an incredible job in raising the most genuine, caring, fun-loving woman I've ever seen. To be able to share my life, my dreams, my bed, and my future with a woman like Becky is nothing short of astounding. And the fact that she considers me the man of her dreams may be even more amazing. Even as an infant, Aubrey always seemed to have a smile on her face and a giggle on her lips. She gets that from her mother, who has placed more smiles on my face than I can even begin to recall.

As for what Aubrey gets from me, well, it's clear that she has my hair and my eyes, and perhaps she also possesses some of my stubbornness. She really doesn't like it when people tell her no. Her "Datty" never really outgrew that stage, either. People have told me—either directly or indirectly—that I couldn't do certain things for as long as I can remember. But their words never stopped me from trying and, in fact, only increased my internal fire. My Vietnamese friends and I were told that we weren't wanted on the youth sports teams in Rockport-Fulton. Yet, by the time I was a senior in high school, my participation on the football team helped to unite what was once a community filled with racial tension. In college, some coaches said I was probably the lone mistake of the 1994 recruiting class. But I finished my career as the leading tackler in the history of Texas A&M University. In the pros, multitudes of skeptics have said I am too small to take the pounding of the NFL game. Yet, one of the game's legendary coaches has said that I could play for him in any era.

I'd love to continue proving the skeptics wrong for years to come. I really thought the Cowboys had turned the corner in 2003, and we were on the verge of becoming playoff regulars and Super Bowl contenders. But instead of building on the success we had enjoyed in 2003, we took a major step backward in 2004. We began the '04 season at 2-1, but then went 4-9 the rest of the way to finish 6-10 overall. Injuries hurt us; mistakes killed us; and a few key losses prevented us from ever making a serious playoff push. It was an extremely frustrating season for me personally, although I did have one of my better years statistically. I recorded 134 tackles and a career-best three interceptions in '04. Nevertheless, the losing wore on my teammates and me. During one particularly miserable stretch, we lost to the Bengals, Eagles, and Ravens by a combined score of 105–34.

It was during that demoralizing skid, however, that Becky informed me she was pregnant with our second child. How's that for an attitude-adjusting message? I went from gloomy to giddy in a matter of seconds. Having children has been a blessing beyond my wildest expectations, and I am so grateful to be able to come home each day to people who don't care if I missed a tackle or whether we won the game or not. Aubrey doesn't care how I played; she just wants me to be ready to play with her. What an amazing, perspective-altering gift this is to Becky and me.

Don't get me wrong, though. Football is still very important to me, and I believe Bill Parcells and Jerry Jones will make the necessary moves to get the Cowboys back into playoff contention. I know for a fact that I am resolute on making my final years in the NFL my most successful ones.

I could envision playing out the remainder of my contract (which runs through the 2007 season), and, depending on what time of year you ask me, I could even see playing beyond that. I would love to etch my name in a prominent place among the Cowboys' triumphant history and possibly collect a Super Bowl ring or two. I am also prepared to handle whatever comes my way. I don't necessarily need a Super Bowl ring to underscore my football career. My hands and fingers are so beat up and twisted that I can't even wear the rings I already own. Besides, if the NFL's express elevator drops me off tomorrow on the basement level, I will walk away from the game with no regrets and plenty of gratitude for the opportunity I received to fulfill what many would have labeled an incredibly farfetched dream. From refugee boats to America's Team, it's already been an amazing—and even miraculous—journey for me. I cannot even put into words how thankful I am for the numerous people—all those mentioned in this book and many more who were not—who have propelled me and inspired me along the journey, but I thank God every night for every one of them.

Most of all, though, I thank God for the manner in which He has used me. My ultimate destination is not the NFL, but rather, one day to join Him. I hope I have been able to use the spotlight of the NFL to reflect His glory. I don't know what God has in store for me in the future. Maybe I'll become a coach for a private, Catholic school. Maybe I'll be able to test-drive fast cars and write reviews for an automotive magazine. Or maybe I'll be a stay-at-home father and the "Soccer Dad" for my kids. Wherever I am and whatever I do, I hope my children will always look at me and be inspired to follow their dreams and believe in miraculous possibilities.

If the son of a pint-sized immigrant shrimper can become the starting linebacker for the Dallas Cowboys, surely all things are possible. I'll always remind my children of that. I'll also remind them that, whenever adversity inevitably strikes or self-doubt enters their minds, to look to their father for strength and inspiration. Not me, mind you, but rather, their heavenly father. I am where I am today because of God's grace and guidance. I've been blessed; I've been lucky; and I've worked to develop my God-given talents to realize many of my dreams.

My life thus far has been an exciting journey; an elevator ride of highs and lows, starts and stops. Whenever a door has closed, another has quickly opened. I've pushed some of the right buttons and been backed into a few corners, as well. Booker T. Washington once said, "Success is not measured by where you are in life, but by the obstacles you've overcome." I wholeheartedly agree. Roadblocks, detours, breakdowns, wrong turns, critics, skeptics, and cynics are all a part of anyone's life. They've certainly been part of mine. The key for me in overcoming obstacles has always been to keep my focus on my ultimate destination. My motto, my life's directional path and my long-term goals can probably all be summarized in two words: Cowboy, up.

Acknowledgments

I remember first mentioning to Dat Nguyen the possibility of writing a book about his life during the spring of 1997. Dat laughed. "Who in the world would want to read that, Rusty?" he asked. I told him that I, for one, would love to read it, and that I would be honored to help him write it. Fortunately, I finally convinced him that his story, along with his faith, attitude, perspective, outlook, and determination, could serve as an inspiration to others. I should know. I consider Dat one of my heroes. His jersey hangs in my son's room; a painting of him hangs in our family's home office; and an action shot of him is on the wall of my office inside Kyle Field.

I have admired Dat's courage and tenacity ever since the first time I watched him play. It wasn't until I really grew to know him, though, that I realized what a remarkably unique young man he is in so many other ways that his football fans rarely see. He's a great Christian witness, a devoted husband and father, and a loyal and genuine friend. I consider it an honor to call Dat my friend, and I love the fact that my son pretends he is Dat Nguyen whenever he plays backyard football games against his dad. I thank Dat for opening up his home, sharing his inner thoughts, making time in his schedule, and driving from one end of the state to the other while he told me his story. I even thank him for hooking me on sushi, which I once thought would never happen. The only stumbling block we continually ran into during this project was Dat's humility. The man often refuses to admit there is anything special about him—on or off the football field. Well, buddy, the whole world now has an opportunity to find out what a one-of-a-kind person you really are, and I am grateful that you chose me to tell your story.

I'd also like to thank Dat's wife, Becky, for her perspectives throughout the book. The word "awesome" comes up every time I attempt to describe Becky to others. Her comments, memories, and laughter helped to complete this book—just as she has completed Dat's life. When we first started doing interviews for the book, Becky and Dat were practically newlyweds, a couple of kids cutting up and poking fun at each other as the tape recorder rolled. They are still doing that, but now they share their giggles with a super kid of their own. Dat and Becky value their private, family time, so it was an honor to be included in some of those moments.

Thanks to all of Dat's other family members, as well. Thank you to his mom and dad for sharing their photos and memories and making certain I never left Rockport with an empty stomach. Thank you to all of his brothers and sisters, especially Ho, who was able to paint a word picture of what it was like to escape from Vietnam and start from scratch in a new country. Thanks to Dat's many friends from Rockport for their contributions to the book and to Big Jimmy and Glenda Hattenbach for the impact they had on Dat's life and on this book. Thanks to all the coaches who helped to shape Dat's football career and filled in the blanks for this book, especially Cliff Davis, Phil Bennett, and Mike Clark.

To Dan Campbell and Rich Coady, thanks for all the stories—the ones printed here and the ones intentionally left out. Some locker room stories are best left in the locker room. Thanks to Homer Jacobs, editor of *12th Man Magazine,* for assigning me to do that feature story in 1997 that started this all, and to the magazine's superb design and graphics specialist, Trey Wright, for all the photo scans and support. Thanks to the Texas A&M video lab, especially Shawn Eyre and Andy Richardson, for turning video tape into pictures for us to consider for the book. Thanks to Joe Nolan for working behind the scenes to secure a foreword from the great Darren Woodson, and thanks to "Woody" for his insights on Dat.

Special thanks to *12th Man Magazine* photographer Kevin Bartram, as well as *Dallas Cowboys Weekly* and Scott Agulnek of the Dallas Cowboys' Public Relations Department, for the football action photos in the book.

Finally, thanks to the world's most beautiful and encouraging editor: my wife, Vannessa. Not only has she read and re-read every word in this book, but she also put up with all the late nights and early mornings when it was being written. Thanks, "V," for all of your efforts, your support, and your patience. Ditto to my kids: Payton, Kyleigh, and our third child, who, as I was putting the final touches on this manuscript, was as active inside Mom's tummy as Dat ever was at middle linebacker.

This was a fun project for me, primarily because I am so sold on the subject matter. After seeing what Dat has accomplished in the first thirty years of his life, I can't wait to see what the future holds for him.

Rusty Burson

Index

Maroon Out, 163

Marshall, Steve, 141

Martin, George, 207

Martin, Harvey, 14

Mary Branch Elementary School (College Station), 139

Maxwell, David, 113

Mekong Delta, 32

Meyers, Phillip, 93, 94

Michigan, 52, 53, 58, 86–88; Ann Arbor, 86–88; Detroit, 86; Kalamazoo, Michigan, 51–54, 55

Michigan, University of, 83–87, 91, 95, 115, 116; Wolverines, 86, 87

Middle Tennessee State University, 115, 116

Minnesota Vikings, 188

Mississippi, 55

Mississippi, University of, 105

Missouri, 70; Saint Louis, 166

Missouri, University of, 165

Mitchell, Brandon, 108, 126

Mitchell, Keith, 108, 113, 114, 123, 126, 170

Moehler, Gary, 85–87

Monday Night Football, 185

Monk, Art, 14

Morris, Sammie, 127

Moss, Randy, 188, 189

Muscle & Fitness (magazine), 102

Napalm, 17, 32

National Liberation Front, 17

NCAA, 85, 155, 165

New England Patriots, 206, 211

New Mexico, 49

New Orleans Saints, 14, 126, 170, 171

New York Giants, 24, 172, 185, 186, 193, 206, 210

New York Jets, 154, 206

NFC East (Division), 14

NFL, 13–16, 19, 20, 23–25, 47, 50, 98, 108, 111, 120, 123, 124, 126, 131, 150, 154, 155, 170–74, 178,

179, 181–87, 189, 194, 197, 198, 200, 207, 209, 211, 212, 215, 216

NFL Combine, 171

NFL Hall of Fame, 174, 180

Ngo, Chau, 127

Nguyen, Aubrey (daughter), 15, 18, 25, 96, 176, 212–15

Nguyen, Becky (wife), 15, 18, 25, 49, 117, 118–20, 128, 129, 130, 132, 133–35, 142–46, 156, 159, 170, 171, 176, 177, 181, 184, 189–92, 194, 195, 199, 204, 205, 212, 214, 215

Nguyen, Dat, 29, 30, 64, 66, 72, 80, 81, 96, 111, 112, 140, 157, 164, 182, 191, 203

Nguyen family, the, 44–46, 49, 50, 53, 54, 56–58, 70, 86, 96–98, 145, 158, 170, 173, 177, 179, 180, 199, 213, 214

Nguyen, Ho (father), 31, 33–42, 46, 49, 51–58, 71, 97, 98, 177, 199, 213

Nguyen, Ho (brother), 33, 35, 39, 40, 45, 49, 53–55, 61, 139

Nguyen, Hung, 39, 41, 54, 61, 77

Nguyen, LyLy, 61

Nguyen, Smith, 127

Nguyen, Tam "Tammy" (mother), 31, 34, 35, 38, 39, 41, 42, 50, 53, 56, 66, 71, 145, 170, 171, 177, 213

Nike, 16, 17, 19, 23, 25, 164

North Vietnamese Army (NVA), 31, 36–42, 80, 81, 213

Notre Dame, 85, 88

Offshore Inn, the, 56, 57

Ogrean, Dave, 19

Ohio, Canton, 183

Ohio State University, 168, 169; Buckeyes, 168

Oklahoma, 49

Oklahoma, University of, 130, 150, 165, 183

CPSIA information can be obtained at www.ICGtesting.com
Printed in the USA
LVOW13s1612290913

354595LV00004B/11/P